Alternative
Tax Proposals

Alternative Tax Proposals

How the Numbers Add Up

Paul V. Teplitz
Cambridge Research Institute

Stephen H. Brooks
Cambridge Research Institute

Lexington Books
D.C. Heath and Company/Lexington, Massachusetts/Toronto

Library of Congress Cataloging-in-Publication Data

Teplitz, Paul V.
    Alternative tax proposals.

    Includes index.
    1. Income tax—United States. 2. Spending tax—United States. I. Brooks, Stephen H.
II. Title.
HJ4652.T45   1986   336.24′0973   85-19049
ISBN 0-669-11616-5 (alk. paper)

Published simultaneously in Canada
Printed in the United States of America
International Standard Book Number: 0-669-11616-5
Library of Congress Catalog Card Number: 85-19049

The paper used in this publication meets the minimum requirements of American National
Standard for Information Sciences—Permanence of Paper for Printed Library Materials, ANSI
Z39.48-1984.
♾ ™

Contents

Figures

Tables

Preface

his book began as a study for the American Retail Education Foundation on the impacts of tax reforms on the U.S. economy. Its purpose was to fill several gaps in the existing literature on the economics of taxation, by providing:

1. A look at tax impacts on the economy as a whole, rather than just certain industries or interest groups.
2. An emphasis on quantitative, rather than theoretical or philosophical, analysis.
3. Explicit attention to consumption-based taxes, but not from an advocacy standpoint.
4. A discussion in common-sense terms written for readers, such as business-people or congressional staffs, who have a practical grasp of economics.

As with many issues of national policy, public interest in tax reform tends to ebb and flow in cycles, alternating between periods of intense interest and periods of inattention. Interest in specific types of taxation similarly tends to wax and wane at irregular intervals. A good example has been the nation's interest in consumption-based federal taxes. In the early 1970s, the Nixon administration suggested that the United States adopt value-added taxes (VATs) similar to those widely used in Europe. The VAT returned to the public eye in 1979–80 and again briefly in 1984, although by that time, most attention to consumption taxes had turned to another contender, the consumed-income tax.

During the waning phases of these cycles, many observers are tempted to say a particular reform proposal is "dead" and worthy of no further consideration. We believe such a viewpoint is shortsighted. Any subject as basic to a government as taxation is likely to generate recurring proposals for modification, and initiatives for certain basic forms of tax will continue to reappear. As long as major European and other countries continue to employ the VAT, for example, periodic proposals for its adoption in this country are likely. This book is offered in the spirit of identifying and analyzing the impacts of some of the most frequently suggested alternative tax systems.

Any work of this size requires the contributions of many people. Thanks are due to the American Retail Education Foundation and Mr. William Kay Daines, Director of Research, for their sponsorship and continuing interest. We wish to express special thanks to Dr. Lawrence Summers, Professor of Economics at Harvard University, whose ideas, challenges, and thoughts on experimental design were a vital contribution. In addition, he supplied much of the material in chapter 3. Others who deserve mention are Christopher Caton and Jesse Abraham at Data Resources, Inc., Josh Chernin and Barbara White at CRI, and James Bryant, Oliver Holmberg, Nat Kurtz, and Paul Thiemann from the American Retail Education Foundation.

1
Introduction

Since the early 1970s calls for major federal tax reform have been growing steadily, and various administrations have tried to address this problem. In 1977 the Treasury Department issued a major study, *Blueprints for Basic Tax Reform*. Major tax laws were passed in 1977, 1981, 1982, and 1984. However, the calls for fundamental reform continue, and the Reagan administration has issued yet another set of blueprints for major restructuring of the federal tax system.

In one survey after another the public has expressed growing discontent with the federal income tax, primarily on the grounds that it is unfair and too complicated. The annual survey conducted by the Advisory Council on Intergovernmental Relations (ACIR) finds that 35 percent of the people rate the federal income tax as the least fair of their taxes, and if the federal government had to raise additional revenues, less than one-fourth of the people would favor doing so by way of the income tax system. Economists, too, have expressed concerns about the present income tax, arguing that it distorts many economic choices, thereby reducing the efficiency of the U.S. economy. Finally, with the rise of supply-side economic thinking, there are many economists and businesspersons who believe that the current tax system is biased against savings and investment and thus contributes to the problems the United States faces in competing in international markets.

For businesspersons trying to understand current tax reform proposals, there is little help in much of the literature on tax reform for two reasons. First, many of the writings are theoretical arguments among professional economists, with little in the way of empirical evidence to prove or disprove the theories. They offer few, if any, quantitative calipers or yardsticks for gauging the significance of their arguments. Much of this literature leaves a lay reader with the uneasy suspicion that the arguments are, "Interesting. True, maybe, but probably not very important in the scheme of things." Equally unhelpful are the advocacy arguments of various interest groups who claim that the sky will fall if their favorite tax break is eliminated. Inherently, these writings have a narrow focus, relating to the specific tax provisions involved. Thus, they yield little insight into the workings of the tax system as a whole.

The purpose of this book is to cut through the theoretical and advocacy arguments to give a sense of proportion to the likely effects of the major proposed tax reforms on the U.S. economy. The focus is economic. The design of any tax system involves many value judgments and political choices. We will not attempt to sort out these choices or take a position on them. Rather, our objective is to compare, side-by-side, the major tax alternatives being considered and to project quantitatively their likely impacts on the U.S. economy.

The tools available for studying the effects of taxes are limited, making the task difficult. One reason the arguments concerning tax reform have remained theoretical and hypothetical for as long as they have is a scarcity of empirically proven theories. Many phenomena basic to the formulation of a tax system are not well understood, for example:

The supply response of savings to after-tax yields.

The supply response of labor to after-tax wage rates.

The amount of *new* business investment induced by specific tax incentives.

The extent of "tax arbitrage" by individuals, for example, borrowing money to put in tax-free IRA accounts.

The extent of the underground economy and other forms of tax evasion.

The amount of business investment moved overseas by U.S. companies because of the tax system.

How much the tax system contributes to higher costs of capital in the United States than in some other countries.

Even such a basic concept as the effect of income and taxes on people's consumption behavior still presents many mysteries for economists. At best, the economic tools for designing tax systems could be characterized as imperfect and still in considerable flux. Much of the knowledge economists have on these subjects has been learned only in the past few years.

In our study of the effects of various tax proposals, we employed one of the principal tools available to economists for empirical analysis, namely, computer simulation models. In particular, we used the Data Resources, Inc., macroeconometric model of the U.S. economy to help quantify the analyses of different tax systems. By using this model to test the effects of each tax program on such macroeconomic variables as GNP, consumption, investment, and foreign trade, we can add a better sense of scale and proportion to the current discussions of tax reform.

We have avoided such details as what happens to the windfall profits tax or the residential energy credit. Although these specific tax provisions may have strong behavioral and economic consequences for their individual sectors, most are tiny in relation to economic aggregates and do not fall into the arena of basic structural reform. The tools of *micro*economic rather than *macro*economic analysis are more appropriate for discussion of such provisions.

In the remainder of this chapter we present background material on specific concerns with the present tax system, the degree of public discontent with the income tax, and a brief history of U.S. tax policy and tax rates. Chapter 2 describes and compares the provisions of major tax alternatives currently under consideration, such as the modified flat tax, the value-added tax (VAT), the consumed-income tax, and excise taxes. This chapter also presents some of the major arguments for and against each tax.

Chapter 3 presents the economic arguments for a move toward consumption-based taxes and the use of the tax system to stimulate investment, along with a review of what economic evidence is available on that subject.

Chapter 4 presents the methodology of the simulation tests we conducted, and chapter 5 analyses the findings. Chapter 6 presents a summary and conclusions.

Concerns with the Present Federal Income Tax[1]

The 1977 Treasury Department study, *Blueprints for Basic Tax Reform*, stated the case for reform:

> There has been increasingly widespread dissatisfaction in the United States with the Federal tax system. Numerous special features of the current law, adopted over the years, have led to extreme complexity and have raised questions about the law's basic fairness. Many provisions of the code are, in effect, subsidies to certain types of taxpayers, or to particular interests, for some forms of investment and consumption. These subsidies are rarely justified explicitly and, in some cases, may even be unintentional. In many instances, they alter the pattern of economic activity in ways that lower the value of total economic output.
>
> The confusion and complexity in the tax code have led Secretary of the Treasury William E. Simon to suggest that the Nation should "have a tax system which looks like someone designed it on purpose." (p. 1)

Blueprints then went on to spell out in specific detail two alternative reforms for replacing the federal income tax. The first was a *comprehensive income tax* that eliminated most deductions, credits, and exemptions, and substituted a set of lower, less steeply graduated tax rates (a broadened, flattened income tax). The second was a *cash flow* tax, or a consumed-income tax, that allowed taxpayers to deduct from income all net additions to savings or investment, but required that they add to income any net withdrawals from savings.

The years since publication of *Blueprints* have been busy ones for changes in federal tax policy, with a significant set of tax reductions later in 1977, the Reagan tax cuts in 1981, and tax increases coupled with partial reforms in 1982 and 1984. Each of these changes has moved the federal tax system somewhat closer to the ideals enunciated in *Blueprints*. Yet much pressure remains for a fundamental restructuring of federal taxes.

Concerns with our present federal tax system can be classified into two groups, economic and social. *Economic* concerns relate primarily to the distortions that taxes may introduce into peoples' economic behavior or to tax-induced biases that reduce the overall strength of U.S. industry and affect its ability to compete with industries in other countries such as Japan. In recent years, much of the economic criticism of the tax system has centered on savings and capital formation.[2] *Social* concerns relate primarily to public perceptions of unfairness and needless complexity in the current tax system. Press reports of a growing underground economy and the rapid growth in tax shelter schemes lead many honest taxpayers to feel that they are shouldering an unnecessarily large tax burden, while dishonest people and the rich get a free ride.

Distortions of Economic Choices

When tax considerations induce a corporation to hoard surplus cash or to enter into dubious mergers and acquisitions rather than pay greater dividends to its shareholders, its behavior is being distorted and the efficiency of the nation's economy is reduced. Similarly, when individuals buy larger homes than they really need or buy expensive boats or foreign cars because they are tax deductible, the tax system is leading to choices that may be inefficient for the economy as a whole. Economists refer to this problem as an efficiency loss.

A few efforts have been made to quantify the efficiency loss in the U.S. economy due to the operation of the federal tax system. The measures are necessarily imprecise and different researchers have obtained differing results, but a practical estimate would be in the range of a few percent. In other words, the nation's GNP might be four to six percent higher if the tax-induced inefficiencies were corrected. This may not seem like much until compared to the 1981 recession, the deepest in postwar history, that represented a slowdown of only about five percent.[3]

A second economic concern with the current tax system is its bias in favor of consumption and against savings and investment. This bias manifests itself in at least two ways:

1. All consumer interest is deductible, even though the items purchased, for example, TV sets, refrigerators, recreational vehicles, or vacations in the Caribbean, generally represent consumption and not investment.

2. Earnings from financial investments, such as stocks and bonds, are fully taxed while the services (earnings) received from investments in owner-occupied houses and consumer durables are not taxed at all.

Indexing for Inflation

Until passage of the Economic Recovery Tax Act (ERTA) in 1981, the federal income tax made no effective provisions for inflation. During the 1970s, millions of taxpayers became familiar with the negative effects of "bracket creep" as their cost-of-living pay increases pushed them into higher and higher tax brackets.

During times of inflation, an unindexed income tax has a tendency to treat the earnings from capital even more harshly than the earnings from labor, further discouraging investment and capital formation. During inflation, interest rates can be considered to include two components: (1) an inflation premium, which represents a return of capital in order to maintain equivalent purchasing power, and (2) a real interest rate. For a savings account or bond investor in the 50-percent tax bracket, the tax system actually confiscates his capital whenever the inflation premium is larger than the real interest component, a condition that existed often during the 1970s and early 1980s. Similarly, business depreciation allowances are understated during times of inflation, resulting in overtaxation of earnings from business investments (or, again, actual confiscation of capital).

The 1981 law now provides for indexing of tax brackets for individual taxpayers, offsetting most of the problem of bracket creep. However, the law still makes no provision for indexing of earnings from capital. Thus, investment and capital formation still are disproportionately taxed.

Overall Treatment of Capital Income

Despite these flaws, it would be inaccurate to portray the current tax system as unfriendly to capital income. The overall tax rate on *real* capital income is relatively low, about 28 percent in 1979.[4] Many features in the present system ameliorate the tax treatment of capital income, for example, investment tax credits, special rates for capital gains, the personal dividends exclusion, exemption of imputed rents on owner-occupied houses, exemptions for pension plans and IRA accounts, and various forms of accelerated depreciation.

The problem is that these tax preferences are both uneven and complicated. Some forms of capital income are lightly taxed, others heavily taxed, leading to dubious schemes to shift income from one category to another (an element in many tax shelters). The large number of regulations and volume of paperwork that go with administering this structure invites public distrust and cynical comment. Even the Treasury Department has referred to the 1976 Tax Reform Act as the "Lawyers and Accountants Relief Act" (*Blueprints*, p. 1). Efforts to plug loopholes only compound the regulations and paperwork. The 1984 Tax Act will add over a thousand pages to the tax code.[5]

One economic flaw in the current tax system that most economists consider to be without redeeming merit is the double taxation of corporate dividends. This double tax is considered to be at the root of a long list of ills, for example:

Corporations unnecessarily hoarding earnings.

Undue reliance on debt instead of equity financing, with consequent increases in companies' financial risks.

Deterrence to the corporate form of doing business.

Unwise corporate investments to avoid earnings payouts.

Complex tax-avoidance schemes for closely held companies.

Many economists would simply do away with corporate income taxes altogether on the grounds that corporations don't consume; their earnings should be taxed to their ultimate beneficiaries, the shareholders. Another approach would be to allow corporations to deduct from income any dividends paid to shareholders. Despite the antipathy of professional economists toward the corporate income tax, many legislators feel that its removal would cause widespread feelings of unfairness and would be politically unacceptable. In any event, corporate income taxes have declined steadily as a share of federal revenues from about 24 percent in 1960 to about 6 percent in 1983.[6]

Political and Social Concerns with the Income Tax

Social concerns with the income tax system relate primarily to public perceptions of unfairness and needless complexity. The annual surveys of ACIR, mentioned above, show a continuing high level of public concern with the fairness of the income tax. Moreover, when people are asked what would be the best way to increase federal revenues, less than one-fourth chose the path of increasing income tax rates. More than half said that a national sales tax would be a preferable way to raise revenues. A continuing theme in these surveys is a feeling that the best way to make the federal tax system fairer is to make upper-income taxpayers pay more, primarily through the elimination or reduction of loopholes.[7] (Tables 1-1, 1-2, and 1-3 set forth the results of these surveys in more detail.)

There is, however, a certain inconsistency to people's responses to different surveys. For example, a 1982 Louis Harris-*Business Week* poll found that 62 percent of Americans favored a single 14-percent income tax rate with nearly all deductions eliminated. When asked which deductions should be scrapped in order to lower the tax rate, 80 percent favored keeping the medical expense deduction, 71 percent favored keeping the home mortgage interest deduction, 66 percent favored keeping the charitable contributions deduction, and large majorities favored keeping other major deductions as well.[8]

Table 1-1
Advisory Council on Intergovernmental Relations Survey on Changing Public Attitudes toward Taxes
(in percent)

Worst or Least Fair Tax	1983	1982	1981	1980	1979	1978	1977	1975	1974	1973	1972
Federal income	35	36	36	36	37	30	28	28	30	30	19
State income	11	11	9	10	8	11	11	11	10	10	13
State sales	13	14	14	19	15	18	17	23	20	20	13
Local property	26	30	33	25	27	32	33	29	28	31	45
Don't know	15	9	9	10	13	10	11	19	14	11	11

	Federal Income	State Income	State Sales	Local Property	Don't Know
1983: Worst or Least Fair Tax					
Total	35	11	13	26	15
Under 35	33	15	13	25	14
Over 65	27	6	11	32	23
High school incomplete	29	9	14	27	22
College graduate	41	13	10	27	9
Under $15K	30	10	14	25	21
$40K+	48	10	11	26	6
Professional; manager; owner	40	14	11	30	5
Blue collar	36	11	12	27	13
1972: Worst or Least Fair Tax					
Total	19	13	13	45	11
30–39	22	16	15	40	10
60+	13	9	10	51	17
Less than high school completed	17	11	13	43	16
Some college	19	13	17	45	8
Professional; manager (average)	19	14	17	44	7
Blue collar	20	13	11	43	14
Under $5K	16	9	13	48	15
$15K+	19	13	14	46	8

Note: Question not asked in 1976.

Table 1–2
Public Attitudes on Ways to Raise Taxes, 1972 and 1983
(in percent)

1983: If the federal government has to raise taxes substantially, what is the best way to do it?

	Increase Individual Income Taxes	New National Tax on Everything But Food	Don't Know
Total	24	52	25
Under 35	26	52	22
Over 65	21	44	35
High school incomplete	19	47	35
College graduate	37	46	17
Under $15K	22	47	32
Over $40K	26	58	17
Professional; manager; owner	29	53	18
Blue collar	20	55	25

1972: If the federal government has to raise taxes substantially, what is the best way to do it?

	VAT	Raise Individual Income Tax Rates	Cut Deductions, Reduce Special Capital Gains Treatment	Don't Know
Total	34	10	40	16
30–39	33	12	41	14
60+	31	10	32	27
Less than high school completed	29	9	37	25
Some college	36	13	42	9
Professional; manager (average)	39	10	39	12
Blue collar	30	10	41	19
Under $5K	30	9	37	24
$15K+	38	9	43	10

Table 1–3
Public Attitudes on Ways to Make Taxes More Fair, 1983
(in percent)

1983: Which single change would make the nation's tax systerm more fair?

	Increase Taxes on Upper Income People	Reduce Taxes on Lower Income People	Make Business Pay More Even if It Results in Fewer Jobs	Leave System Alone	None of the Above	Don't Know
Total	49	13	6	16	7	9
Under 35	46	15	8	16	6	10
Over 65	41	14	4	22	5	14
High school incomplete	42	14	6	20	3	16
College graduate	57	8	5	13	12	5
Under $15K	45	15	6	16	5	13
Over $40K	43	11	7	17	17	5
Professional; manager; owner	54	11	5	15	11	4
Blue collar	49	16	8	16	5	6

Inconsistencies such as these suggest a large component of measurement error in these public surveys. In answering the survey questions, many respondents may not be considering (or fully aware of) the consequences of tax reform for their personal finances. Few respondents appear ready to give up their own favorite aspects of the current system, be they home mortgage interest deductions, tax shelters, or any of the other special provisions in the present code.

This pattern of popular support for the *concept* of major tax reform but strong opposition to the specifics of such reform has led many observers to say that only a thorough overhaul that would eliminate nearly all deductions and loopholes is politically feasible. Congress would then be able to say no to *all* interest groups rather than saying yes to some and no to others. Such an approach, however, demands a high degree of political discipline, and many seasoned veterans question whether it is realistic. For example, Rep. Barber Conable, ranking Republican on the House Ways and Means Committee, has observed that the concept of a broader tax base with lowered marginal rates "will not easily . . . be translated into legislative action. . . . Let's be realistic in our expectations."[9] In further discussion with one of the authors he commented,

> "Many businesspeople seem to have the idea that we can pass a tax reform, once and for all, and then leave it alone. That doesn't seem very likely unless we also elect a new breed of congressmen who are less accessible and less responsive to their constituents. . . . One of the prices people pay for taxation with representation is complexity."[10]

While the logic on both sides of this issue is persuasive, legislative history certainly is on the side of Rep. Conable and others who forecast incremental changes rather than a massive reform. Nevertheless, during personal interviews in Washington, D.C., we were told by a number of experienced observers of tax politics that the momentum for tax reform is greater now than it has been in many years. There appear to be two main driving forces behind this momentum: (1) the need to "do something" to at least set the stage for future tax increases to reduce deficits, and (2) the general movement toward deregulation and less government interference with the day-to-day operations of the private economy. Whether or not massive reforms result from the current movement, these two forces are likely to be a continuing influence on tax legislation in coming years.

The Business Community

As with consumers, fairness of the current tax system is of major concern to the business community. Although individual interest groups may attack various provisions of the Internal Revenue Code or propose new concessions from time to time, the most commonly voiced objection of the business community to the current tax system is the wide variation in effective tax rates among corporations.

While some companies pay close to the statutory 46-percent rate on their earnings, other companies—especially those in certain industries (for example, capital-intensive ones)—pay much lower or even negative effective rates. For example, in 1983 the five largest companies in the paper and wood products industry *as a group* had an effective U.S. tax rate of -0.5 percent, and a worldwide effective tax rate of only 7.2 percent.[11] A list of major industries and their effective tax rates for 1980–1983 is presented in table 1–4. The ten largest retailers had moved downward from 34.1 percent in 1980 to only 20 percent in 1983. However, some members of the retailing industry contend that these figures are distorted by the very low effective rates of Sears, Penney's, and Household International, whose tax rates were reduced by their financial services subsidiaries, and that together represented a large portion of the retailing industry. For most retailers, these observers believe, the effective rates were closer to the earlier figure. Even the 20-percent level, however, was higher than the overall average of 16.7 percent of all 218 companies in all industries.

Despite these concerns, the business community has given only modest support to the idea of major tax reform. A 1977 survey of CEOs of major companies, conducted by the accounting firm Touche Ross & Co., found that only 30 percent of the respondents wanted tax simplification and 83 percent preferred income taxes to some form of consumption tax (see table 1–5). Sentiment in favor of tax reform has probably increased since that time but still is not high. Various reports have indicated a growing interest in a national sales tax or a value-added tax, particularly by executives within large, capital-intensive industries who are concerned that any reforms of the income tax will diminish the special breaks they received in the 1981 tax legislation. Thus, the sales tax or VAT is favored not for its own merits, but as a way of heading off unfavorable changes to the corporate income tax.

A Brief History of Federal Taxation

Much of the government's revenue in the years after the Revolution was supplied by tariffs. In 1795 tariffs accounted for 91 percent of the government's revenue; this figure fluctuated between 75 percent and 90 percent for the next fifty years.

Until about 1820, the government saw tariffs strictly as a source of revenue. However, as trade between the United States and other countries increased, the government came to use tariffs as a protectionist measure as well as a source of revenue. Tariffs on some products exceeded 50 percent—and sometimes even 100 percent—of the price of the product itself. As late as 1885, tariffs accounted for over 55 percent of the government's receipts.

Government revenue rose slowly and steadily but was marked by sharp upward swings in times of war. Because deficit spending was frowned upon, the

Table 1–4
Effective Tax Rates for Selected Industries
(in percent)

Industry	1980	1981	1982	1983
Aerospace	16.4	6.8	-.6	14.0
Airlines	3.0	Loss	Loss	Loss
Beverages	28.0	28.8	20.5	18.7
Broadcasting	n.a.	n.a.	8.9	18.5
Chemicals	13.7	5.0	-17.7	-1.0
Computers, office equipment	24.9	25.3	26.4	26.3
Construction	n.a.	n.a.	15.9	.7
Electronics, appliances	24.5	17.1	14.3	7.4
Financial institutions	5.8	2.7	-3.8	6.4
Food processors	35.6	26.8	31.6	25.9
Glass, concrete	n.a.	n.a.	Loss	17.5
Instruments	37.1	26.6	21.9	32.8
Insurance	n.a.	n.a.	-6.3	9.9
Investment companies	n.a.	n.a.	21.3	9.3
Metal manufacturing	15.2	10.2	Loss	Loss
Metal products	n.a.	n.a.	30.2	15.1
Mining	n.a.	n.a.	Loss	Loss
Motor vehicles	n.a.	n.a.	Loss	3.5
Paper, wood products	-1.4	-14.2	36.1	-.5
Petroleum	31.1	21.7	18.2	21.3
Pharmaceuticals	39.2	35.9	32.7	27.2
Railroads	10.7	-7.5	4.1	3.3
Retailing	34.1	22.3	20.4	20.0
Rubber	n.a.	n.a.	39.0	19.6
Soaps, cosmetics	n.a.	n.a.	33.3	35.6
Telecommunications	n.a.	n.a.	1.6	4.8
Tobacco	31.4	31.3	36.3	33.8
Trucking	37.5	46.1	36.9	34.5
Utilities (electric, gas)	10.9	10.3	15.6	7.1
Wholesalers	n.a.	n.a.	36.1	34.8

Source: Joint Committee on Taxation, *Study of 1983 Effective Tax Rates of Selected Large U.S. Corporations* (Washington, D.C.: Government Printing Office, 1984).

Notes: n.a. = not available.

Negative tax rates indicate that the industry received a refund.

No tax rate is calculated for industries with losses.

Table 1–5
Touche–Ross Survey of Sample of Fortune 500 CEOs, 1977

83 percent would rather have income taxes than consumption taxes

49 percent chose income tax for reason of political reality

79 percent said tax system should be used to induce economic behavior as well as to collect revenues

94 percent favored eliminating double taxation of corporate earnings

72 percent saw favorable treatment of capital gains as an incentive to capital formation

30 percent demanded simplification of the tax code

government usually raised existing taxes and levied new ones during wartime. During the War of 1812, for the first time, small income taxes and estate duties were imposed, but both were repealed after the war.

The revenue needs of the government again rose during the Civil War. In addition to raising tariffs and excise taxes, the government passed a mildly progressive income tax in 1861. However, it was a full year before the tax was even levied and, in the confusion of the war and its aftermath, administration of the income tax was poor and evasion was easy. The income tax was repealed in 1871, even though it had accounted for almost 20 percent of the government's revenue during its life.

It was also during the Civil War period that the first death taxes and capital gains taxes (on purchase and sale of property held less than one year) were enacted. They were repealed in 1871 and 1872.

There were no significant federal tax changes for the next twenty-five years. However, during that time a strong single tax movement grew. Led by populist Henry George, proponents called for a single tax to be levied on the economic value of land regardless of whether improvements had been made. Single-taxers believed that this would discourage speculation, decrease land prices, and provide enough revenue so other taxes could be eliminated. Although George died in 1897, others (Tom Johnson, Lincoln Steffans) carried on the fight, and Woodrow Wilson had several ardent single-taxers in his administration. However, the idea died during the First World War for several reasons: (1) there were internal schisms between single-taxers who agreed with George's other philosophies and those who did not. These differences widened after George's death; (2) the single tax also lost its separate identity as its proponents got caught up in other movements (women's rights, anti-imperialism); (3) there were bitter splits among single-taxers over what the U.S. role in the World War should be; and (4) many people felt that the progressive income tax made the single tax on land—as an instrument of taxing the wealthy—unnecessary.

By the late 1880s and early 1890s, popular support for a progressive income tax grew as stories about great individual fortunes were circulated. In 1894, a progressive income tax was passed as an amendment to a tariff bill. Although politicians had professed support for a progressive income tax, the real impetus for the tax was supplied by southern antiprotectionists who wished to enact the income tax as a substitute or partial substitute for tariff revenues. (Since the South was largely an agrarian economy, there was little support for protectionist measures; tariffs were supported by northern industrialists.) In 1895, however, the federal income tax was declared unconstitutional by the Supreme Court.

To help finance an expensive war with Spain, the government levied a new round of taxes in 1898, including an estate tax, an inheritance tax, and increased tariffs and excise taxes. Oddly, much of the impetus for the death taxes came from Andrew Carnegie, who argued that it was unfair to pass on wealth from generation to generation. The inheritance taxes were repealed in 1902.

In 1909 the forerunner of the modern corporate income tax was passed. Called a "tax on the privilege of doing business," it was directly proportional to net income. By calling it a "privilege" tax, however, the government was able to survive several challenges to the tax on constitutional grounds. This tax exempted the first $5,000 of net income and taxed the remainder at 1 percent.

At about the same time, popular support again grew for the individual income tax, and in 1913 the Sixteenth Amendment was passed. Opposition came from the wealthy, who maintained the income tax was socialistic, but tremendous support for the tax came from poor- and middle-income persons, who felt the tariffs and excise taxes (both consumption-based) were regressive.

Barely seven months after this amendment was ratified, individual incomes were subjected to a tax. There was a $3,000 exemption (which exempted the large majority of the population from paying any tax). Marginal rates ranged from 1 percent to 6 percent, but effective rates were extremely low. For instance, the effective rate for a family with four exemptions earning $20,000—an extraordinary sum in those days—was only 0.8 percent. The maximum marginal rate of 6 percent was imposed only on incomes over $1,000,000 (see table 1–6).

Individual and corporate rates and the government's dependence on them rose dramatically from about 1915 to 1920. By 1920 the highest marginal income tax rate was up to about 70 percent. The sharp rate increases of this period were caused by World War I. During this same period, individual and corporate income taxes accounted for about 70 percent of government revenues.

During the 1920s, however, Harding, Coolidge, and later Hoover, lowered income taxes substantially. Much of the impetus came from Andrew Mellon, Secretary of the Treasury, of whom it was said that "three Presidents served under him." These reductions and the depression lowered government receipts from income taxes very quickly; by 1932 only 38 percent of government revenue was being derived from income taxes.

Inheritance taxes of the present type were first levied to help finance World War I. In 1924 a gift tax was added, and both taxes have continued since then. The capital gains tax was revived in 1913 as part of the individual income tax. It was based on the purchase and sale of real estate within a twelve-month period; the gain was subject to regular income tax rates. Beginning in 1924, the taxpayer could elect to pay capital gains taxes at a rate of 12.5 percent. In the 1930s the scope of assets subject to capital gains taxes was expanded and a new temporal base was established. Assets held for less than one year were recognized at 100 percent, with the scale of recognition running down to 30 percent for assets held ten years or more.

During the 1940s, income tax rates rose dramatically to finance the war effort. Marginal rates at the top bracket reached 90 percent, and, for the first time, taxpayers with as little income as $600 were subject to tax. Rates fell somewhat in the late 1940s and early 1950s and remained relatively stable until the Reagan tax cut and the dropping of the highest marginal tax rate from 80 percent to 50 percent.

Table 1-6
Effective Tax Rates, Four Exemptions
(in percent)

Net Income Group	1970	1965	1960	1955	1950	1945	1940	1935	1930	1925	1920	1915
$600	—	—	—	—	—	0.5	—	—	—	—	—	—
$1,000	—	—	—	—	—	1.5	—	—	—	—	—	—
$2,000	—	—	—	—	—	2.3	—	—	—	—	—	—
$3,000	2.3	2.8	4.0	4.0	3.5	9.2	—	—	—	—	0.8	—
$5,000	7.5	7.7	10.4	10.4	9.0	15.1	1.5	1.0	0.2	0.2	2.1	0.2
$6,000	9.1	9.2	12.0	12.0	10.4	16.8	1.9	1.4	0.3	0.3	2.6	0.3
$8,000	11.6	11.6	14.4	14.4	12.7	19.8	3.1	2.3	0.5	0.5	4.2	0.5
$10,000	13.2	13.0	15.9	15.9	14.2	22.5	4.4	3.4	0.8	0.8	5.6	0.6
$15,000	16.3	16.1	19.3	19.3	17.4	28.4	7.5	5.5	1.9	1.9	8.0	0.7
$20,000	18.9	18.5	22.3	22.3	20.2	33.9	10.7	7.3	2.9	2.9	9.8	0.8
$25,000	21.2	20.8	25.1	25.1	22.7	48.8	14.3	9.3	4.0	4.5	11.4	1.0
$50,000	32.4	31.7	37.8	37.8	34.3	53.7	27.5	17.2	9.1	9.7	18.3	1.5
$100,000	44.8	43.7	51.9	51.9	47.2	68.6	42.9	30.2	15.7	16.0	31.2	2.5
$1,000,000	68.6	66.9	85.5	85.5	79.1	90.0	71.7	51.1	24.1	24.1	66.3	6.0

Source: U.S. Bureau of the Census, *Historical Statistics of the U.S. to 1970*, p. 2. Washington, D.C., p. 1112, Y 412–439.

Table 1-7
Postwar Federal Tax Legislation

Act	Annual Revenue Gain or Loss (billions of dollars)
Revenue Act of 1948	-5.0
Revenue Act of 1950	4.6
Excess Profits Tax Act of 1950	3.3
Revenue Act of 1951	5.7
Internal Revenue Code of 1954	-1.4
Excise Tax Reduction Act of 1954	-1.0
Federal-Aid Highway Act of 1956	2.5
Revenue Act of 1962	-0.2
Revenue Act of 1964	-11.4
Excise Tax Reduction Act of 1965	-4.7
Tax Adjustment Act of 1966	none
Revenue and Expenditure Control Act of 1968	10.2
Tax Reform Act of 1969	-2.5
Revenue Act of 1971	-8.0
Tax Reduction Act of 1975	-22.8
Tax Reform Act of 1976	1.6
Tax Reduction and Simplification Act of 1977	-8.6
Revenue Act of 1978	-18.9
Crude Oil Windfall Profit Tax Act of 1980	12.2
Economic Recovery Tax Act of 1981	-162.1
Tax Equity and Fiscal Resp. Act of 1982	27.0
Highway Revenue Act of 1982	3.7
Number of acts with net revenue Increases: 9 Reductions: 12	
Cumulative Amount of Changes[a]	$-175.8

Source: *Annual Reports* of the Secretary of the Treasury, and *General Explanations* of revenue acts by the Joint Committee on Taxation.

[a]Because of inflation, the year-to-year amounts are not directly comparable. This total is included only as an indicator of the direction of changes made by these acts.

Table 1-7 gives a recapitulation of postwar U.S. tax legislation. Except for temporary measures to help finance the Korean and Vietnam wars, most of these measures represent efforts to stimulate the economy, implement national policies to encourage certain industries, or offset the effects of inflation.

Notes

1. Throughout this discussion, we will focus on the federal income tax system. Social Security taxes, tariffs, excise taxes, and the like are not generally considered part of the current discussions of tax reform.

2. Barry P. Bosworth, *Tax Incentives and Economic Growth* (Washington, D.C.: The Brookings Institution, 1984), see especially chapter 1.

3. Don Fullerton, John B. Shoven, and John Whalley, "Replacing the U.S. Income Tax with a Progressive Consumption Tax: A Sequenced General Equilibrium Approach," *Journal of Public Economics,* 20 (1983):3–23.

4. Eugene Steurle, "Is Income from Capital Subject to Individual Income Taxation?" *Public Finance Quarterly,* July 1982:290–292.

5. Paul Craig Roberts, "Only a Bold Stroke Can Cure Deficit Hysteria," *Business Week,* 11 June 1984:16.

6. Office of Management and Budget, *Federal Government Finances: 1985 Budget Data* (Washington, D.C.: Government Printing Office, 1984).

7. Susannah E. Calkins, *1983 Changing Public Attitudes on Governments and Taxes,* Report S-12 (Washington, D.C.: ACIR, 1983).

8. This pattern has been repeated in a number of surveys as recently as early 1985. See, for example, "Down on the Levy," *Wall Street Journal,* 12 December 1984.

9. Barber B. Conable, "Before We Leap Into Tax Reform," *Wall Street Journal,* 7 December 1984.

10. Telephone conversation with Rep. Conable, August 26, 1985.

11. Joint Committee on Taxation, *Study of 1983 Effective Tax Rates of Selected Large U.S. Corporations* (Washington, D.C.: Government Printing Office, 1984).

2
The Major Tax Proposals

A s occurs with many legislative movements, numerous variants of tax reform have been proposed or introduced as bills in Congress. On closer examination, however, the proposals for reforming the federal tax system divide themselves broadly into two categories according to their objectives.

1. Those that seek to improve public trust in the tax system. These proposals, which frequently include such terms as "tax simplification," "fairness," and "improved compliance," are responsive to the opinion polls that show widespread public discontent with the complexity and perceived inequities in the current federal income tax. Example proposals include the so-called "modified flat tax" being considered by the Reagan administration, the Bradley–Gephardt Fair Tax, and the Kemp–Kasten Fair and Simple Tax.

2. Proposed reforms that seek to strengthen economic growth and U.S. competitiveness in international markets. These reforms, which often mention such benefits as "capital formation" and "consumption-based taxation," are responsive to concerns by many economists, businesspersons, and others about the long-term slowdown in U.S. economic growth and reduced competitiveness of U.S. industries against industries of other countries such as Japan. Examples include Rep. Cecil Heftel's consumed-income tax, the value-added tax (VAT), a national sales tax, and added taxes on energy usage.

These two types of reform are not necessarily opposed to each other, and many people would like to see elements of both adopted.

In this chapter, we examine the rationales for these different proposals along with some of the arguments for and against each type. The chapter also contains reviews of a number of issues common to almost any federal tax reform proposal. Appendix 2A contains brief descriptions of several specific tax reform proposals and their major provisions.

Tax Simplification

As discussed in chapter 1, much of the current dissatisfaction with the federal tax system arises out of its complexity and a widespread feeling that many people are taking advantage of the complexity to pay much lower rates than they should. Thus, a number of reforms have been proposed, including one by the Treasury Department, to reduce the complexity of the income tax, lower its rates, and reduce the opportunities for tax avoidance. (Brief descriptions of the Bradley–Gephardt and Kemp–Kasten tax simplification proposals can be found in appendix 2A.)

Most goals of these proposals would be accomplished by a sharp reduction in the number of deductions, exemptions, exclusions, and credits in the current income tax. This broadening of the tax base theoretically could add as much as 90 percent to the income subject to taxation, which in turn would permit a reduction in rates. Elimination of deductions would also reduce record-keeping for the average taxpayer and close many loopholes. Proponents also claim that the resulting lower tax rates would reduce incentives for tax evasion, further improving the tax base.

Opponents of tax simplification (besides those trying to protect their special treatments in the present law) also contend that there is little evidence in the history of Congress to suggest that it would keep its hands off any new tax system once installed. More so than the legislatures in other countries, the U.S. Congress has tended to deal with the tax laws at a detailed level.

A second criticism of tax simplification is that it is simply a wolf in sheep's clothing, a ploy to increase revenues without raising rates back to the politically unacceptable levels of the 1970s. When push comes to shove, the argument goes, the promised rate reductions of a Bradley–Gephardt or Kemp–Kasten tax will not be delivered. Or, if they are passed initially with lower rates, the political temptation to raise rates back up to near current levels within a few years will be irresistible.

Yet another group of critics suggests that the simplification of a new tax system may be illusory. Complexity in the current tax system arises primarily from three sources: (1) the inherent complexity of an economy as large and diverse as that of the United States, (2) special favors and concessions introduced by Congress, many of them for worthy and popular goals, such as broadening home ownership, preserving historic buildings, and helping single-parent families, and (3) "dynamic complexity" that accumulates year by year as taxpayers and tax attorneys seek new loopholes and tax administrators find new ways to plug them. All three sources are reinforced by strong political traditions of taxpayers seeking relief in both Congress and the courts. Sweeping away the current complexities, these critics contend, would simply begin anew the process of creation.

The issue of tax simplification is plagued by a lack of empirical data to support or disprove the assertions being made in connection with various proposals. For example, many observers make the common-sense statement that lower tax rates should reduce incentives for tax avoidance and cheating. Yet we have been unable to find empirical evidence to support this belief. Tax rates have been cut substantially since 1977, which seemingly should have reduced tax shelter activity. Exactly the opposite has occurred. It now appears that the growth of tax avoidance and tax sheltering are rooted in more fundamental phenomena, such as two-income households, growing public financial awareness, insurance firms and stockbrokers seeking new markets as their old ones become more competitive, and increased concerns about financial security during old age.

In summary, it is important to recognize that tax simplification responds mostly to political concerns rather than economic ones. There are no economic tests of how much simplification is enough, and little, if any, empirical evidence by which to judge the extent of alleged problems. The choices boil down to value judgments and response to public opinion. Several points, however, should be kept in mind:

1. The current push for rationalization and simplification has its roots in the broader political climate that favors less government intervention in private affairs.

2. This suggests that the political costs of arguing for the retention of special tax favors may be high.

3. Long-standing legal and political traditions are almost certain to lead to a considerable degree of complexity in any tax system, reflecting to some extent the underlying complexity of the U.S. economy.

4. Lower rates and a simpler tax code may reduce sheltering and avoidance behavior somewhat, but they are unlikely to reverse the long-term trend toward more tax-conscious behavior of the public.

From an economic standpoint, each specific provision of a tax simplification proposal needs to be separately considered. However, none of the changes proposed (and likely to pass) in connection with tax simplification are likely to have dramatic effects on the economy as a whole, despite the possibility of significant effects in a few specific sectors.

Tax Changes to Stimulate Savings and Investment

The two principal tax proposals that encourage more savings and investment are the VAT and the consumed-income tax. Both operate by shifting the tax base toward consumption instead of income.[1] The VAT would be applied as an additional tax, retaining the present income tax system, whereas the consumed-income tax would be a replacement of the present system. Their advantages and disadvantages can be summarized as follows.

VAT

Advantages

1. VAT is a broad-based tax and therefore a powerful revenue raiser ($10 to 20 billion per point).
2. Largely self-policing. Difficult to evade.
3. Can be integrated with the income tax to offset any tendency toward regressivity.

Disadvantages

1. Inflationary. Increases price levels and thus would trigger many cost-of-living escalators.
2. VAT's revenue-raising power can be a dangerous temptation toward future increases in government spending.
3. Requires new tax collection and administration system, in addition to existing system.

Some critics of the VAT point to the strong defeat that Congressman Al Ullman received for his 1980 proposal to partially replace the Social Security tax with a VAT. They argue that this defeat (and Ullman's subsequent defeat in the 1982 congressional elections) proves that this country would not accept a European-style VAT. This conclusion may be invalid, however, because many circumstances surrounding that bill muddied the waters. In a number of ways the bill was oversold, and some proponents asserted benefits that were implausible or simply untrue.[2]

CONSUMED-INCOME TAX

Advantages

1. Eliminates tax-induced distortions in consumption, saving, and investment. Strong "carrot" for increased saving.

2. Collection and administration would be similar to the present income tax and could be handled by existing apparatus.

3. Can have any desired degree of progressivity.

Disadvantages

1. Transition from current tax would be very difficult, for example, with separate recordkeeping for old and new assets.

2. Increases somewhat taxpayers' recordkeeping.

3. Could have a tendency to concentrate wealth, unless offset with appropriate inheritance and gift taxes.

The idea of a tax on consumption rather than income traces at least as far back as Thomas Hobbs and, consequently, John Stuart Mill. Its basic appeals are its encouragement of thrift and its taxation of what people take *from* the economy rather than what they put *in*. The consumed-income tax is fundamentally a more radical approach to stimulating savings than any of the other tax proposals currently under consideration. A full changeover to this type of tax would require a massive task of identifying every taxpayer's "old" and "new" (or "qualified" and "nonqualified") assets. Also, over the course of a taxpayer's lifetime, a consumed-income tax would shift his tax burden somewhat from his prime earning years to his nonearning years, for example, adolescence, college years, and retirement. Such a shift is felt by many to run against the grain of popular preference.[3]

Both of these consumption-based taxes would be relatively free of the problems of indexation for inflation found in the current tax system. The VAT is an *ad valorem* tax that rises or falls in proportion to prices, and the consumed-income tax effectively eliminates taxes on capital income, which are the source of most such problems.

Direct consumption taxes, such as the VAT, the sales tax, and excise taxes, share a number of characteristics in common. By themselves, they tend to be regressive since they collect the same amounts from taxpayers regardless of income. Most proposals would offset this tendency with some form of credits or other concessions in the income tax for low-income persons. However, this device isn't perfect, and there remains always a possibility of adding to the tax burden of persons who can least afford it. Second, most such taxes would require new administrative machinery for collection, a prospect that may not be appealing in the current antigovernment political climate. Finally, as chapter 3 will discuss, these proposals for consumption-based taxation rest on appealing but relatively unproven economic theory.

Basic Issues in Any Tax Reform

Efforts at tax reform face basic problems, inherent in any taxation of a modern economy, that limit the degree to which the reforms can approach the ideals toward which they strive.

Size and Complexity Issues

One of the largest impediments to tax reform is the sheer size and complexity of the U.S. economy. Any effort to simplify tax regulations faces a difficult environment in which the natural forces of politics, persuasion, human error, and litigation seemingly lead one step backward for every two steps forward. The tax system must be workable in day-to-day operation for approximately a hundred million individual taxpayers and almost three million corporations, plus numerous partnerships, trusts, and other entities. In this environment, even minor oversights or imperfections in the new tax rules can affect large numbers of taxpayers. Major reforms, therefore, are likely to require a process of ironing out details that takes several years.

Multiple and Offsetting Reactions

Reactions to tax change are seldom uniform. One person's tax incentive may be another person's disincentive or penalty. Two examples from current topical issues will illustrate the problem:

1. *Labor supply* A major concern with the present tax system is that its steeply progressive rates may be discouraging people from work. However, a cut in those rates could have either of two effects. For some people, the extra after-tax income now available may be just the incentive they needed to seek additional work. For others, the extra take-home pay from their current work may cause them to ease up and enjoy the benefits of the tax cut in the form of more leisure time. Still others may simply choose to enjoy the extra money and not change their work habits at all. Various economists have attempted to measure these patterns, and the general conclusion is that tax rates have relatively little effect on the work hours of males with dependents. However, other groups, particularly married females, are more sensitive to the tax rates. On balance, the studies suggest that a cut in rates would increase the labor supply, but not as dramatically as many tax reform proponents assert.[4]

2. A similar pattern applies to the potential effects of tax cuts on people's *savings behavior*. If after-tax yields are increased, some people may be motivated to set aside a larger fraction of their income. Others, who are saving toward a specific goal such as a retirement income or a down payment on a house, may choose to save less, since the higher net yields will make up for smaller annual contributions. Empirical evidence in this area is less well developed than for labor

supply. Consumer saving behavior has not been strongly sensitive to yields, but appears to be becoming more so. One area in which there is clear evidence of rate sensitivity is *dissaving,* that is, consumer borrowing to finance major purchases such as cars and appliances. An increase in the after-tax cost of this borrowing clearly would result in less borrowing and, therefore, a net increase in private saving in the economy.

Boundary Definitions

Surrounding any tax are a set of boundary questions, for example:

Are fringe benefits, such as health insurance, considered part of taxable income?

Are "payments in kind," for example, free flights for airline employees, considered part of taxable income?

How should barter transactions be taxed?

Is an expensive painting on an executive's office wall a luxury or a legitimate business expense?

In a large, complex economy a myriad of such questions must be answered, requiring administrative machinery to develop specific answers and resolve disputes. Also, these boundaries, representing grey areas of the law, offer continuing opportunities for lawyers and aggressive taxpayers to challenge the tax system. Indeed a small industry has arisen in the United States to help taxpayers probe these boundaries of the tax system and fully exploit any new concessions. Examples include tax accountants and attorneys, numerous publications, a weekly front-page column in the *Wall Street Journal,* membership organizations, and, more recently, computer software.

Obviously, one way to reduce the extent of the boundary-definition problem is to reduce the number of boundaries, that is, to have fewer deductions, credits, exemptions, and other forms of special treatment for certain categories of taxpayers. The various tax simplification proposals currently being considered are based on this idea. However, one consequence of simplification is loss of flexibility, such as for handling hardship cases or truly exceptional cases (the executive who runs an art gallery probably *can* justify that expensive painting on his wall as a genuine business expense).

A second approach to reducing boundary issues was used by Congress in the 1982 and 1984 tax laws. This is called *threshhold raising* and involves setting the conditions for certain deductions or other special treatments high enough to eliminate, statistically, the great majority of taxpayers. Thus, taxpayers can now deduct medical expenses only if those expenses exceed 5 percent of their gross income. The Treasury Department's proposal would add additional thresholds.

Shifting across Boundaries

When a tax system has lower rates for one category of income than for another, taxpayers will be motivated to shift income into the favored category in order to take advantage of the lower rates. In the present tax system, the most popular devices are (1) shifts among family members, for example, gifts to children, Clifford Trusts, or putting children on the payroll of small businesses, (2) shifting income forward into future years, for example, by deferred compensation arrangements, use of retirement programs, or investment in equipment-leasing tax shelters, and (3) shifting from ordinary income into capital gains, for example, when people sell their homes for a premium price but offer low-cost second mortgages to the buyers.

One of the principal arguments in favor of tax simplification is that this incentive for income shifting will be greatly reduced. If the highest marginal tax rate was 30 percent, as in the Bradley–Gephardt proposal, and the lowest rate 14 percent, many taxpayers may not feel the 16 percent savings worth the inconvenience and risks of trying to shift their income across categories. This proposition remains untested, however.

Shifting to consumption taxes such as a VAT simply changes the arena for the category-shifting problem. For example, if food and medicines were exempted from a VAT, as is often suggested, manufacturers and retailers would be almost certain to begin efforts to have their products reclassified into the favored category whenever a plausible argument could be made for doing so, as illustrated by some of the boundary-definition questions discussed earlier.

Appendix 2A

Bradley–Gephardt/Fair Tax Act of 1983

Chief Proponents: The bill is considered the Democratic party's rallying point for tax reform.

House of Representatives: Anthony, AuCoin, Barnes, Bates, Beilenson, Berman, Boxer, Brown, Carr, Coelho, Coleman, D'Amours, Dwyer, Evans, Fazio, Ferraro, Flippo, Frank, Frost, Gephardt, Hughes, Kaptur, Kogovsek, Levine, Long, Lowry, Lundine, McNutty, Minish, Moody, Morrison, Panetta, Patterson, Pease, Reid, Sabo, Sikorski, Staggers, Tallon, Valentine, Wheat, Wirth, Wise, Wolpe.

Senate: Baucus, Biden, Bingaman, Bradley, Dodd, Hart, Kennedy, Lautenberg.

Date Introduced: June 9, 1983

Principal Tax Features

I. Rates

Marginal Rate	Single Taxpayers	Married Persons Filing Jointly
14%	Up to $25,000	Up to $40,000
25%	$25,000–$37,500	$40,000–$65,000
30%	Over $37,500	Over $65,000

II. Anticipated Revenue

In the first year it is expected that the Fair Tax Act of 1983 will bring in approximately the same amount of revenue as does the current tax structure.

In future years, it is claimed that there is hidden revenue-raising potential that would take effect due to the rising revenue cost of preferences.

III. How Collected?

Same as under current tax system.

IV. Definition of Amount to Be Taxed

The Bradley–Gephardt bill would broaden the base of individual and corporate income taxes by expanding the definition of taxable income and by repealing the majority of tax preferences.

    A. Taxable income would include

        1. Tier two railroad retirement benefits.

        2. Amounts paid by an employer for group-term life insurance.

        3. Unemployment compensation.

        4. Annual increase in the cash surrender value of life insurance policies.

        5. Interest on industrial development bonds and mortgage subsidy bonds.

        6. Amounts contributed by an employer to accident and health plans.

        7. Gain from sale of principal residence.

        8. Capital gains, taxable at the 30 percent rate.

        In addition, the bill treats transfer of corporate stock in payment of a debt at the fair market value of the stock.

        Provides limited exclusion from income for scholarships and fellowships.

    B. Amount for Personal Exemption

        1. Individual taxpayer, spouse filing separately = $1600.

        2. Individual head of household = $1800.

    C. Amount of Standard Deduction

        1. Individual taxpayer, spouse filing separately = $3000.

        2. Joint return, surviving spouse = $6000.

    D. Rate-reducing Repeals

        1. Tax tables for individuals.

        2. Minimum tax for tax preferences.

3. Personal service corporations.

4. Special averaging rules for lump-sum distributions.

5. Accumulated corporate surplus.

6. Personal holding companies.

7. Income averaging.

8. Graduated corporate tax rates.

9. Indexation of tax rates.

E. Base-broadening Repeals

1. General tax credit

2. Investment tax credit

3. Possession tax credit

4. Elderly and disabled tax credit

5. Contributions to public office candidates tax credit

6. Home purchases tax credit

7. Residential energy conservation tax credit

8. Producing fuel from a nonconventional source tax credit

9. Alcohol used as fuel tax credit

10. Increasing research activities tax credit

11. Employee stock ownership tax credit

12. Clinical testing for ownership tax credit

F. Exclusions Repealed

1. Partial income tax exclusion for interest and dividends.

2. Qualified transportation furnished by an employer.

3. Cafeteria plans furnished by an employer.

4. Dependent-care assistance programs

5. Dividend reinvestment in public utilities.

6. Payments to encourage mining for defense purposes.

7. Earned income of citizens living abroad.

8. Certain allowances.

9. Income from sources within the United States.

10. Income from sources within Puerto Rico.

G. Deductions Repealed

1. Two-earner married couples.

2. Adoption expenses.

3. State and local personal property and sales tax.

4. Intangible drilling and development costs for oil and gas wells.

5. Depreciation.

6. Amortization of pollution control facilities.

7. Improvements made by lessee on a lessor's property.

8. Certain depreciable assets.

9. Amortization of reforestation expenditures.

10. Percentage depletion.

11. Development expenditures.

12. Mining and exploration expenditures.

13. Long-term capital gains.

14. Increase the floor on the deduction for medical and dental expenses from 5 percent to 10 percent.

V. Allowances/Deductions/Exclusions

Can be applied only against the 14 percent rate.

1. Deduction for household and dependent care expenses.

2. Exemption of $1,000 for dependents.

3. Deduction for home mortgage interest.

4. Deduction for charitable contributions.

5. Deduction for state and local income and property taxes.

6. Deduction for payments to IRA, Keough plans.

7. Deduction for individuals and corporations for depletable property determined as a percentage of the balance in a recovery account for each year.

8. Exclusion of veteran's benefits.

9. Exclusion of social security benefits.

Fair and Simple Tax (FAST)

Senate Bill 2600
House Bill 5533

To reduce tax rates in a manner that is fair to all taxpayers and to simplify the tax laws by eliminating most credits, deductions, and exclusions.

Proposed by: Senator Robert Kasten (R-Wis.)
Representative Jack Kemp (R-N.Y.)

April 26, 1984

A "Fair and Simple Tax" (FAST) has been introduced to the House and Senate. It proposes to overhaul the federal income tax by eliminating most deductions, exempting most working poor, and imposing a flat-tax rate. The bill doubles the personal exemption, increases standard deductions, and protects wage earners by shielding 20 percent of wages and salaries from taxation. FAST is the Republican alternative to the Democratic flat-tax proposal by Bill Bradley and Richard Gephardt. It was expected to be the rallying point for tax reform in the 1984 GOP convention.

Principal Tax Features

I. Rates

Personal Income Tax: 25 percent
Corporate Income Tax: 30 percent

II. Anticipated Revenue

"Neutral." The proposal would raise revenue equal to about 12 percent of GNP, the same as the current combination of corporate and personal income taxes.

III. How Collected?

Same as under current tax system.

IV. Base

A. Personal Income Tax

1. Gross income less employment income exclusion

Includes special allowance for wage and salary earners

excludes 20 percent of gross income from taxation for those making up to $39,300 on additional income the exclusion gradually decreases, disappearing on income above $102,000

individuals with employment income of less than $10,000 ($20,000 in the case of a joint return) are excluded from tax.

2. Unemployment compensation

3. Annual increase in cash surrender of life insurance policies

4. Amounts contributed by employers to accident and health plans.

B. Corporate Income Tax

1. Capital gains are fully taxed, the rate will be reduced from 28 percent to 20 percent

2. The basis for capital gains would be indexed for inflation

3. FAST allows for full deduction and carry-forward for capital losses

4. Small businesses receive a tax rate of 15 percent of taxable income that does not exceed $50,000 and can expense up to $10,000 of business investment

V. Deductions/Exclusions/Allowances

A. Personal exemption

FAST doubles the current exemption, allowing $2,000

B. Standard Deductions

Joint return/surviving spouse = $3,500
Single/head of household = $2,700
Married/separated = $1,750
In any other case = -0-

General interest payments
Home mortgage interest payments
Real property taxes
10 percent of medical and dental expenses
Charitable contributions
Payments to IRA, Keough Plans, and other retirement pensions
Benefits provided for by employer
Foreign-source income
Employee business expenses
Depreciation
Moving expenses

Capital losses of individuals deductible in full; carryover of excess of such loss over gross income is allowable

Scholarship and fellowship exclusion limited to tuition and related expenses

C. Rate-reducing Repeals

Tax tables for individuals
Personal service corporations
Special averaging rules for lump-sum distributions
Accumulated corporate surplus
Personal holding companies
Income averaging
Graduated corporate tax rates

D. Base-broadening Repeals

Investment tax credit
General tax credit
Elderly and disabled tax credit
Public office contribution tax credit
Home purchasers tax credit
Residential energy conservation tax credit
Producing fuel from a nonconventional source tax credit
Alcohol used as a fuel tax credit
Increasing research activities tax credit
Employee stock ownership tax credit
Clinical testing for certain drugs tax credit

E. Exclusions/Exemptions Repealed

Partial income tax exclusions for interest and dividends
Qualified transportation furnished by employer
Dividend reinvestment in public utilities
Payments to encourage exploration, development and mining for defense purposes
Mortgage subsidy bonds
Exemption for certain private purpose bonds
Exemption for taxation of deposits and withdrawals from the Capital Construction Fund

F. Deductions Repealed

State and local taxes
Unused investment credit

Two-earner married couples
Adoption expenses
Improvements made by lessee on lessor's property
Start-up expenditures
Intangible drilling costs
Percentage depletion
Development expenditures

Consumed-Income Taxes

H.R. 4442
Progressive Consumption Tax Act of 1983:, Introduced by Rep. Cecil Heftel (D-Hawaii), on November 17, 1983.

Basically, the bill taxes consumption rather than income, using the following brackets:

Taxable Consumption	Marginal Rate
Under $2,000	None
$2,000–$5,000	10 percent
$5,000–$8,000	12 percent
$8,000–$12,000	14 percent
$12,000–$16,000	16 percent
$16,000–$22,000	20 percent
$22,000–$28,000	25 percent
$28,000–$35,000	30 percent
$35,000–$50,000	35 percent
$50,000–$100,000	40 percent
$100,000–$150,000	45 percent
Over $150,000	50 percent

(These rates are not contained in H.R. 4442 but will be in an amended bill yet to be introduced.)

The bill proposes to include in gross income:

All compensation, rent, royalty, dividends, alimony, annuities, and so forth.

Unemployment compensation, social security, pensions.

Gifts, inheritances, prizes.

The cost of group-term life insurance provided by employers to the extent that it exceeds the employee's contribution.

Net increases in indebtedness or net decreases in savings would be taxable. The personal exemption would be raised to $2,000. The amount of the unified tax credit against estate tax (currently $192,800) would be repealed.

Because the tax bracketing is somewhat flatter than the current structure and because the tax base (consumption) is smaller than the income tax base, there is considerable base broadening envisioned by this bill.

Credits for foreign taxes would be repealed. The deduction for interest paid would be limited to that interest related to business or investment activity. The tax deduction for real and personal property taxes would be eliminated. The bill limits the maximum deduction for charitable contributions to 5 percent of gross income.

There are a myriad of additional repeals, including:

Deductions

Sections 167, 168 (depreciation, Accelerated Cost Recovery System [ACRS])
Section 189 (amortization of real property construction period interest and taxes)
Section 1202 (capital gains)

Credits

Sections 38 and B. IV. A. 1 (investment in depreciable property)
Section 44C (residential energy credit)

Exclusions

Sections 101, 102 (death benefits, gifts, inheritances)
Section 103 (interest on government obligations)
Section 108 (income from discharge of indebtedness)
Section 116 (partial exclusion of dividends)
Section 121 (one time exclusion of gain by sale of residence by person over 55)
Sections 911, 931, 933 (earned income of persons living outside of the United States)

No proposed tax rate on corporations has yet been set by Heftel and his staff; it will be included in the amended bill. The *tax base* of the corporation would be the excess (if any) of:

50 percent of the firm's net income, over the dividends paid during the taxable year

Note: The above is a description of one consumed-income tax proposal. Many tax observers and much of the academic materials on consumed-income taxes assume that the corporate income tax would be eliminated entirely.

Presumably, the effect on the economy would be to increase the pool of savings, lower interest rates, and encourage investment and capital formation. Consumed-income taxes would try to remove the bias toward spending and away from savings that the current tax system (aided by inflation) has inherent in it.

Value-Added Tax

Currently in proposal form by Charls Walker
American Council for Capital Formation

Previously proposed to House of Representatives by House Ways and Means Chairman, Al Ullman, 1980

Proposal: A tax levied at each stage of the production process, the bill would impose a Value-Added Tax (VAT) on sales of property and services at each stage of the production and distribution process, including the retail stage in order to scale back the corporate and individual income tax.

Principal Tax Features

I. Rate

Businesses would pay a net tax equal to 10 percent of the value of property or services sold. The tax would be included in the price that a business charges its customers.

II. Anticipated Revenue

The Congressional Budget Office estimates a 10 percent VAT could yield \$160–\$260 billion annually (at 1984 income levels) depending on the comprehensiveness of the base.

III. Tax Base

With a consumption-type VAT such as adopted by the EEC, the VAT tax base is the firm's gross sales less its purchases of inputs including capital equipment from other firms. Generally, the taxable amount is the price charged for property or services.

A. Taxable Transactions

1. The added value of products or services is equal to the cost the company incurs for the labor and capital it uses in its production activity subject to certain adjustments, depending on the particular VAT employed.

2. Taxable transactions include the sale of property in the United States, the performance of service in the United States, and the imparting of property by a taxable person in a commercial transaction. They can be calculated as the total payments made to a firm's productive process.

3. To calculate the value-added tax liability, a firm applies the tax rate to its sales in order to obtain its *gross tax liability*. The firm

subtracts the taxes paid by suppliers (shown on invoices) from gross liability, yielding a *net tax liability* figure.

4. With deductions the base is equivalent to *consumer spending* and thus a consumption tax.

B. Deductions

1. Firms incur no tax liability on the purchase of intermediate goods because they receive credit for VAT paid in previous transactions. Thus, a taxpayer would receive a credit for VAT paid on purchases of capital items as well as for VAT paid on purchases of supplies and services.

2. Wages paid are considered costs of inputs

3. Immediately deducts from base the purchase price of newly acquired capital assets (repeals depreciation)

4. Rebates VAT on exports

C. Exemptions

1. Savings and investment income

D. Exclusions Proposed (or deduction possibilities)

1. Food and nonalcoholic beverages
2. Medical care
3. Nonretail sales of farmers and fishermen
4. Mass transit in urban areas
5. Government sales of property or service (some exceptions)
6. Earnings from capital

E. Exempt Organizations

1. Transctions of charities' educational activities of public and tax-exempt educational institutions.

2. The bill provides special rules for real property, interest transactions and insurance companies.

F. How Collected?

1. The VAT is assessed to businesses on a monthly transactional payment basis with the use of invoices to claim VAT credit, and on a direct basis to consumers upon purchases.

National Retail Sales Tax

Currently in proposal form by Charls Walker
American Council for Capital Formation

Proposal: Among a wide array of tax reform and deficit reduction proposals being studied by the Treasury Department is a National Retail Sales Tax. The tax on goods and services would be levied at the retail stage and consist of a percentage of the selling price of those products when purchased by the consumer.

Principal Tax Features

I. Rate

Depending on the form, the tax could vary between 10 percent and 20 percent.

II. Anticipated Revenue

Estimates indicate a comprehensive 10 percent sales tax would yield about $260 billion at 1984 income levels.

III. Tax Base

The base for a national sales tax would be the aggregate amount of retail sales in the United States. Thus it would be a consumption tax.

IV. Deductions/Exemptions/Credits

A. Exempts savings and investment income

B. Exempts necessities—food, medical care. Apply a refundable income tax credit to proverty-line families to compensate for the sales tax on necessities. Apply differential rates to basic versus luxury goods.

C. Deducts educational expenses and charitable contributions.

V. Assumed Economic Effect

The effects of National Sales Tax could be difficult for the economy to absorb. Even with a phase-in period or provisions to exempt certain items from change, there would be shocks to individuals, companies, and the economic system as a whole. Presumably the increased pool of savings and investments would boost the economy; however, it is generally accepted that the tax will cause price hikes and spur inflation.

Tax on Business Transactions (TBT)

Principal Tax Features

The TBT is much like the Value-Added Tax (VAT). Both taxes would levy on businesses a tax on the addition to value made to a product at each step of the process of manufacturing.

The difference between the TBT and VAT is that with the TBT, no tax would be levied at the retail level. Retail sales, finance insurance, real estate, and outlays for personal, educational, and health services would all probably be exempted from the TBT tax base. At all other levels, the TBT would be assessed on the difference between the value of the firm's sales and the value of the purchased inputs and capital equipment used in producing the goods sold.

A TBT would probably be a hidden tax, not passed on to consumers as a tax per se. However, the increased costs (the TBT) incurred at each step of the manufacturing process would certainly be reflected in prices at the retail level. A TBT might at least partially replace the corporate income tax, the individual income tax, or the social security tax. The TBT would probably be rebateable on exports and would probably be imposed on imports.

Currently no comprehensive TBT proposals are being considered by Congress.

Estimates show that each percentage point of a TBT taking place in 1986 would yield $9 billion; by 1992 this could rise to $15 billion, implying that a 15 percent TBT could raise $225 billion. Because the TBT would increase in step with GNP, it would probably provide a more stable base of revenue than income taxes.

Energy Tax Proposals

As part of the effort to reduce the federal deficit, Congress has considered several proposals that would impose additional taxes on energy. Most federal excise taxes are levied on a unit basis (for example, the gasoline and alcohol taxes), or as a percentage of selling prices. New taxes on energy could include both.

The following are examples of the considerations that have been brought forth, most of which are not in active form and studied further as part of the Fundamental Tax Reform report by the Treasury Department in 1984.

I. Ad Valorem Energy Tax

An across-the-board excise tax, based on the selling price of all types of energy consumed in the United States has been considered by the Senate Finance Committee, the Reagan Administration, and the American Council for Capital Formation.

Senate Finance Committee Proposal

Senator Robert Dole (R-Kans.), chairman of the Senate Finance Committee, introduced an energy tax proposal to be included in the deficit reduction plan.

A. Rates

The committee proposal would levy a 2.5–3.0% tax on all forms of energy consumed in the United States including oil, natural gas, natural gas liquids, coal, and electricity.

Tax rates for different commodities would be set for a unit of that commodity—a ton of coal or a barrel of oil, for instance, based on the average nationwide price per unit.

It would be the broadest consumption tax in the federal code.

B. How Collected

The tax would be levied at the easiest collection point in the distribution system, not the user. For instance, the oil tax would be imposed on the sale of refined petroleum products by a refiner while the natural gas tax would be imposed on the sale to a local distribution company.

C. Revenue Effect

The Treasury Department estimates the tax would raise $68.2 billion from 1986 to 1989, according to Department of Energy, Dole's tax plan would take effect if proportionate cuts in federal spending were made.

II. Reagan Administration Proposal

The Reagan Administration considered including a broad-based energy tax as part of a contingent tax increase for inclusion in its FY-85 budget.

A. Rates

Rates included in the FY–84 budget were a three-year standby tax increase to begin in FY–86. It contained provisions for a $5-a-barrel excise tax on domestic and foreign oil and a 5 percent surtax on corporate and individual income. The taxes were to go into effect if the deficit remained above a certain amount, however, the recovery continued and Congress enacted spending cuts.

B. Revenue Effect

Such a tax would raise $96.5 billion from 1986 to 1989.

III. American Council for Capital Formation Proposal

A. Rates

A third energy tax proposal by Charls Walker of the American Council for Capital Formation, would levy a 5 percent Ad Valorem Tax on all energy consumed at either the wholesale or retail level.

B. Revenue Effects

The tax would raise $10.7 billion in 1985 and $82.9 billion over the 1985–1989 period.

IV. Oil Import Fees and Domestic Oil Taxes

A number of proposals seek to tax imported oil and refined products as well as levying taxes on domestic oil producers in addition to the Windfall Profits Tax.

A. Objectives/Advantages

Oil import fees and taxes on domestic oil would be significant revenue raisers and relatively easy to administer. A tariff on imported oil would tend to depress imports, thereby reducing dependence on foreign oil. Higher prices for oil would encourage the substitution of coal, natural gas, and other fuels for oil.

B. Rates/Revenue Effects

CBO estimates that a tax of $2 per barrel could raise $5.7 billion in 1985 and $39.3 billion over the 1985–1989 period.

Oil import Fee Bills currently in the House include:

H.R. 1729	$2.00 a barrel fee
Status	Introduced March 1, 1983, then referred to the Committee on Ways and Means (no action taken)
H.R. 2328	$1.80 a barrel
Status	Introduced March 24, 1983, then referred to the Committee on Ways and Means (no action taken)
H.R. 4915	$.04 a barrel
Status	Introduced February 23, 1984
	Referred to Energy and Commerce Committee February 28, 1984
	Hearings March 1 and March 6, 1984

V. Natural Gas Tax

CBO estimates that decontrol of all natural gas accompanied by an excise tax could raise $5 billion in 1985. Alternatively, a simple excise tax on all gas of 30 cents per 1,000 cubic feet could raise about $3.5 to $4 billion per year or $17.5 billion over the 1985–1989 period.

A. Natural gas decontrol would serve the dual goals of stimulating exploration and promoting conservation by consumers and industrial users. In addition, decontrol would eliminate inequitable discrepancies in gas prices across the country. An excise tax on gas might improve the chances of decontrol being enacted.

VI. Gasoline Tax

The federal excise tax on gasoline, which was raised from $.04 to $.09 in April 1983, could be increased again.

The CBO estimates that increasing the gasoline excise tax by 5 cents per gallon would yield $3.2 billion in 1985 and $20.7 billion over the 1985–1989 period.

VII. Excise Taxes (see provisions in House Bill 4170)

Windfall Profits
Liquor
Cigarettes
Telephone
Highway Use
Diesel Fuel

Objectives/Advantages

Excise taxes are relatively easy to administer.

Relying more on excise taxes and less on income taxes would help reduce the bias against saving and investment in the tax code.

Increasing gasoline taxes is a simple way to raise revenue because the mechanism for collecting the tax is in place. It passes part of the expense of maintaining access to oil on to the driver.

Notes

1. Brief descriptions of the VAT and a consumed-income tax proposal appear in appendix 2A. Also included are discussions of a national sales tax, a so-called tax on business transactions (TBT), and additional excise taxes. For most macroeconomic purposes, a federal sales tax would be functionally equivalent to a VAT, with the principal difference being in its method of collection. The TBT is a VAT that exempts retailers' value-added. Thus, its macroeconomic impacts are similar to the VAT, except that it would require higher tax rates to raise an equivalent revenue. Excise taxes, such as an energy tax, would have similar macroeconomic effects (though smaller) to the VAT or a sales tax. For these reasons, the excise tax, sales tax, and TBT are not treated separately through most of this book.

2. Charles E. McClure, Jr., "Thoughts on a Value-Added Tax," *Tax Notes,* October 22, 1979:539–543.

3. Despite its longevity as an idea, a consumed-income tax has only been tried by two countries—India and Sri Lanka in the late 1950s—as an experimental supplement to the income tax. Both experiments were dropped after short trials. Sri Lanka tried it again briefly in 1976–1977, whereupon the minister of finance called the tax "unworkable and impractical." See Richard Goode, "The Superiority of the Income Tax," in *What Should be Taxed: Income or Expenditure?* ed. Joseph A. Pechman (Washington, D.C.: The Brookings Institution, 1980) 50.

4. Barry Bosworth, *Tax Incentives and Economic Growth,* (Washington, D.C.: The Brookings Institution, 1984) pp. 172–176.

3
Why Some Economists Favor Consumption Taxes

Many economists believe that the government's fiscal, monetary, and regulatory policies during the 1950s and 1960s contributed strongly to the "stagflation" of the 1970s, the declining rate of U.S. economic growth, and the inability of many U.S. industries to compete in international markets. Proposed remedies include a number of measures that have already been implemented, such as deregulation, tighter control of the money supply, lower taxes, and reduced government spending. But many of these economists would like to go further, particularly in the area of taxation, by moving away from the current income tax toward taxes on consumption. As explained in chapter 2, there are two consumption-tax options under consideration: (1) a consumed-income tax that would replace the present income tax, and (2) a national sales tax or VAT that would be added to the existing system.

Since the idea of consumption taxation is new to many people in the United States, this chapter sets forth the economic arguments for consumption taxes, the assumptions on which these arguments are based, and the available empirical evidence to shed light on these assumptions. Our purpose is not to choose sides in the current debate about tax reform, but to explain the thinking behind consumption taxes so that readers can make their own better informed judgments.

Consumption Taxes and Capital Formation

Attaining an adequate rate of capital formation in the United States during the 1980s will be a continuing challenge for economic policy. During the 1960s and 1970s, the U.S. share of GNP devoted to capital formation fell below the levels achieved by most other industrialized nations and below U.S. historical experience. Devoting a larger share of national output to investment, particularly in research, automation, and industrial modernization, would help restore rapid productivity growth and rising living standards.

The Productivity Shortfall

The major concern about the nation's level of investment is the relationship between capital formation and productivity growth. Productivity growth in the United States has decelerated rapidly; between 1948 and 1967 the growth rate of productivity (as measured by output-per-labor hour in the private economy) was 3.1 percent per year as compared to 2.3 percent between 1967 and 1973 and only 0.8 percent between 1973 and 1981.

Consequences of reduced productivity growth for standard of living over the long run are greater than those of any other current economic problem. In 1981 the U.S. economy produced approximately $12,780 worth of output per capita. Had productivity growth continued at the 1948–1967 rate up until 1982, output per capita would have reached $16,128, about 26 percent higher than the actual 1981 level. As a standard of comparison, the recent recession reduced per capita output by only 4 percent, less than one-fifth the reduction attributable to the productivity shortfall. As time passes, the consequences of reduced productivity growth will be compounded. Increasing the productivity growth rate by two percentage points annually would more than double our material standard of living by 2020, compared to the level it would reach otherwise.

The productivity slowdown cannot reliably be attributed to any single cause or simple combination of causes. Contributing factors mentioned by various analysts include higher energy prices, regulatory changes, reduced research and development spending, reduced opportunities for technical innovation, changing demographic composition of the labor force, changing worker attitudes, and reduced capital formation. An accurate accounting of the sources of the slowdown is probably impossible in light of the multitude of competing explanations and the statistical difficulties associated with distinguishing between their relative effects.

Many of the factors causing the productivity slowdown are probably not reversible through public policy. For example, there was little the federal government could have done to offset the negative effect of oil price increases or to influence changing cultural attitudes toward work. However, changing the rate of capital formation is viewed as a principal way in which government policy can help restore productivity growth, and this idea is at the heart of the calls for a movement toward consumption taxation.

Capital Formation and Productivity Growth

Several economic benefits derived from increasing the rate of capital formation are (1) workers have more equipment, on average, at their disposal; (2) new investments reduce the average age of capital stock, so that physical assets embody more recent technological innovations; and (3) technological development tends to accelerate, because the development of more efficient and sophisticated capital goods occurs when the demand for new capital goods increases.

It is instructive to compare the productivity growth rates of different countries with their shares of output devoted to new investment. Although productivity growth and investment rates are simultaneously determined by a multitude of factors, it is striking that a strong positive relationship emerges. As shown in table 3-1, Japan has both the highest investment share and the highest productivity growth rate, while the United States has the lowest investment rate and one of the lowest productivity growth rates.

Table 3-1 also shows that the United States falls behind other major industrial nations in another key measure of net capital formation, namely, the personal savings rate. At times during the 1970s and early 1980s, Japan devoted almost twice the share of its gross domestic product to fixed investment as did the United States. No other major industrial nation devotes as small a fraction of total output to savings and investment as does the United States.

Although the reasons for these large international differences in rates of capital formation are not understood precisely, some evidence suggests that many of the roots may lie in different public policies. After World War II, rebuilding of capital stock was a primary goal of economic policy in continental Europe and Japan. Governments in those countries encouraged saving and investment and disregarded the early Keynesian fear that oversaving might reduce aggregate demand and depress real economic activity.

In contrast, officials in the United States feared a postwar relapse into depression and avoided policies that would encourage saving. For example, some economists advocated sustained budget deficits as a means of absorbing excess private savings. Much of this thinking continued, though in more moderate forms, through the 1950s and 1960s.

Table 3-1
Savings, Investment, and Productivity Growth in Selected Countries (average annual rates, 1979–1983)

Countries	Gross Fixed Capital Formation[a] (percent)	Personal Savings Rate[b] (percent)	Productivity Growth (percent, 1980–1983)
United States	17.7	5.8	3.1
France	20.9	15.5	4.7
W. Germany	21.6	14.2	2.9
Italy	19.2	23.8	2.2
U.K.	16.2	11.9	5.2
Japan	30.6	18.8	6.4
Canada	22.4	13.0	2.2

Source: U.S. Bureau of the Census, *Statistical Abstract of the United States, 1985*, (Washington, D.C.: U.S. Government Printing Office, 1985) p. 435, Table 723, and p. 853, Table 1495.
[a]Gross fixed capital formation as a percent of GNP.
[b]Ratio of savings to disposable personal income, expressed in percent.

It now seems clear—on the basis of four decades of economic experience since the end of the Great Depression—that such fears of secular stagnation caused by a high and rising saving rate were unwarranted. The much greater risk is that productivity growth in the United States will continue to stagnate at low levels and American workers will have to accept a lower rate of growth in their standard of living than their foreign counterparts.

Current Tax Rules and Capital Formation

Many economists believe that the present income tax system encourages consumer borrowing and discourages saving. We discussed in chapter 2 the distortions that inflation causes in the income tax. During the 1970s the combination of tax rules and inflation produced a dramatic decline in the after-tax yields on saving and, at the same time, a large reduction in the cost of borrowing. The tax system therefore accentuated the classic "buy now, save later" behavior that occurs during inflationary periods and thus actually reinforced the inflation itself.

During the 1960s, nominal interest rates on three-month Treasury bills averaged 4.0 percent. With a consumer price inflation rate that averaged 2.3 percent, savers were left with a real pretax return of 1.7 percent. Savers in the 30-percent marginal tax bracket earned a real return of only 0.5 percent after taxes.

However, even this meager return was attractive in comparison with subsequent developments. During the 1970s, while the average inflation rate rose to 7.1 percent, the average interest rate increased to only 6.3 percent. As a consequence, the same 30-percent bracket savers saw their savings *eroding* at a rate of 2.7 percent per year.

At the same time that tax rules have reduced the return on savings, they have encouraged dissaving through borrowing. Because consumer interest payments are tax deductible, taxpayers who itemize their deductions are encouraged to use credit to finance purchases of consumer durables and other goods. As inflation increased during the 1970s, the real after-tax cost of borrowing declined and eventually became negative. Indeed, in the first quarter of 1980, the real after-tax cost of borrowing for a taxpayer in the 30-percent bracket was −1.2 percent. The encouragement of borrowing to finance purchases of durable goods probably reduced the aggregate saving rate substantially during the 1970s.

The tax reforms enacted in 1981 were designed to increase saving. Reductions in marginal tax rates raised both the after-tax yields on saving and the after-tax costs of borrowing. Marginal tax rates for a median-income family, for example, were lowered from 28 percent to 22 percent (beginning in 1984). The marginal tax rate for high income taxpayers, who account for a large fraction of personal saving, was reduced from 70 percent to 50 percent.

Other provisions in the 1981 tax law also were directed specifically at encouraging people to save. Individual Retirement Accounts (IRAs) were extended to cover the entire working population, permitting yearly tax deductible contributions of $2,000. Private estimates suggest a substantial response to this legislation, with about $10 billion placed in IRAs during 1982. A crucial issue in evaluating the efficiency of IRAs is their effectiveness in raising saving incentives on the margin. Some critics argue that IRAs do not provide an *incremental* incentive for saving, because contributors can simply transfer funds from other investments without increasing total savings. While this may occur, it is certainly not universal. According to members of the investment industry, more than half of all IRA account holders contribute less than the maximum amount allowable each year, indicating that they do face increased saving incentives on the margin. Moreover, mutual funds and others in the industry report that their IRA accounts have exceptionally low turnover, in comparison with investors' other accounts. Thus, IRA savings are a relatively permanent addition to the nation's pool of savings.

The 1981 tax act also encouraged saving by reducing the top rate on capital gains from 28 percent to 20 percent. This reform further compensates for the distorting effect, illustrated in chapter 2, of inflation on the taxation of capital gains income. Complete elimination of this distortion would require indexing of capital gains, a feature embodied in the Treasury Department's newest tax reform proposal.

The 1981 tax law left unsolved, however, the overtaxation of interest income caused by inflation. Since a major part of an individual's earnings from savings come in the form of interest, this flaw remains as a significant deterrent to saving. The Treasury's latest tax proposal would resolve the problem by full indexation of interest income.

A lively debate continues as to the effects of the 1981 tax law. The authors of this act as well as many supply-side economists give full credit to these tax changes for bringing about the nation's economic recovery of 1982–1984 and other good things that have happened to the economy since passage of the law, for example, an increased level of venture capital investing. But, the personal saving rate has *not* increased significantly, leading some critics to denounce the law as ill-advised or as a gift to the rich at the public expense.

The most reasonable assessment of the 1981 tax reforms is that it is too early to tell their effects. Many of the law's provisions were not fully phased-in until 1984, and a few provisions remain to take effect. Moreover, consumer's habits tend to change slowly, so it may take five or more years to judge the full effects of this law.

Consumption Taxes

In recent years support has grown among economists and tax experts for taxation of consumption rather than taxation of income. Some advocates support consumption taxation on the grounds that taxing individuals on what they take from the economy is more fair than taxing what they contribute to the economy. A tax system based on consumption might also prove easier to administer than the current system because it would eliminate many of the problems involved in measuring certain types of capital income or in indexing. In the remaining sections of this chapter, we will explore in more detail both the economic growth case and the equity case for consumption taxation, and the assumptions on which these cases rest.

Supply Response of Savings to After-Tax Rates of Return

The traditional view among economists has been that changes in the rate of return are likely to have only a small effect on the saving rate. This consensus is supported by theoretical arguments pointing to the likelihood of mixed reactions of some people saving more (to take advantage of the higher rates) and other people saving less (because higher rates permit them to reach a defined goal with less money set aside from their income). The ambiguous implications of theory are matched by empirical studies that yield conflicting (and generally low) estimates as to the impact of changes in the rate of return. The highest of these empirical estimates suggests only a modest response, for example, a person saving $1,000 per year at 10 percent rates would increase to $1,190 per year if rates went up to 11 percent.[1] This estimate has been widely regarded as being too high.

In recent years, however, a new group of economists has challenged this conventional wisdom. They assert that both the theoretical analysis and empirical evidence demonstrate a strong likelihood that increases in the real after-tax rate of return received by savers would lead to substantial increases in long-run capital accumulation.[2] Under their reasoning, a shift toward expenditure taxation would lead to significant increases in the private savings rate. They argue that the negative findings of traditional empirical approaches result from a methodological failure to distinguish between transitory and permanent changes in the rate of return.

A large number of economists have attempted to estimate the effects of changes in the rate of return on consumption and savings using traditional methods (based on the so-called Keynesian consumption function).[3] No consensus has emerged. Only one economist obtained a statistically significant and substantial positive interest elasticity of savings. However, subsequent research by others showed that his results were extremely sensitive to the choice of sample period and to issues of data construction. Summers and others argue that fundamental conceptual problems make it almost inconceivable that consumption-function estimation can ever answer the questions of interest. Three difficulties seem paramount in their view.

First, when a saver's full life cycle is considered, theory suggests that the value of consumers' endowments will be a direct function of interest rates. Higher rates mean greater wealth passed on to the next generation. These effects were not considered in the earlier studies. When they were taken account of in some simulation studies by Summers and others, strong positive effects of increases in rates of return on savings resulted.[4]

Second, persons concerned with tax policy are interested primarily in the response of savings to *permanent* changes in the real after-tax rates of return. The experiments provided by history have come in the form of largely transitory changes in after-tax rates of return. Both theory and common sense suggest that people will respond less to temporary changes in rates of return than they will to permanent changes. This creates a strong presumption that simple extrapolation of the historical experience will underestimate the response of savings to permanent changes in the rate of return. Moreover, researchers examining past history for long-term phenomena have had to work with data that had a low signal-to-noise ratio. Business cycles, tax law changes, oil price shocks, and similar events have all affected savings behavior, often with effects greater than the one being measured.

Third, there are a standard set of difficulties associated with the consumption-function methodology employed in these earlier studies. Many of the important variables in the models were unmeasurable, and thus were based on assumptions. The modeling of expected future labor income was inadequate. No variables were included to address theoretically relevant issues such as age structure of the population or expected retirement age. In an important 1981 study, Auerbach and Kotlikoff illustrated the behavior of an economy in which savers' life-cycle behavior was fully considered and a number of standard economic parameters relating to savings were estimated. Their results indicated that the parameter estimates of traditional methods were extremely sensitive to the choice of sample period—too sensitive to provide a useful guide to the effect of government policies.[5]

Recent work by a number of economists suggests a new approach.[6] In general it is possible to estimate the parameters of the utility function that drives consumer behavior, even when it is impossible to estimate any kind of traditional consumption function. This can be done using data on individual consumers or, with aggregation assumptions, on aggregate data.[7] Allowance can be made for the possibility that many consumers are liquidity constrained. Once these utility functions have been directly estimated, simulation exercises can be used to estimate the effects of tax reforms. Of course, much more complex analyses, taking account of individual diversity and adding strict information on wage earnings profiles, should be possible as well.[8]

The results of such elaborate simulation exercises cannot be predicted. Preliminary evidence tends to suggest that savings are interest elastic. In the more reliable estimates, Summers found values of the long-term elasticity of savings that clustered at the high end of the range considered. Similar estimates were found using both microdata and macrodata. Also, if proper allowance was made for future growth in the economy, estimated time preference rates were positive, reinforcing the positive effects of rates of return on savings. Future research, particularly using microdata for individual savers, will refine these conclusions and enhance considerably understanding of savings behavior.[9]

Equity Arguments for Consumption Taxation

Beyond the issue of savings and economic growth, many economists maintain that a shift to consumption taxation would increase fairness and equity in the U.S. tax system. Thomas Hobbes argued that there was greater justice in taxing people on what they took from the social pot (their consumption) than on what they contributed (as measured by their incomes).[10] In many cases, this value judgment seems compelling, as for example in the case of a wealthy man who draws down his wealth to maintain a high rate of consumption. Should he not pay some tax? Similarly, the argument goes, a profligate borrower who lives beyond his income should pay taxes on his pleasures.

Critics of consumption taxes point to the apparent counter-example of a miserly millionaire who could enjoy great wealth and power but pay little tax. (Note, however, that any proceeds or interest earned on his wealth would ultimately be taxed if they were spent.)

It is worth dwelling on this argument for a moment. A consumption tax is, in a sense, less coercive than an income tax. Under an income tax, persons who earn and save must pay tax. In the words of an old joke, "The reward of energy, enterprise, and thrift is taxes." Under a consumption tax, enterprise and thrift would not be penalized, and even energy and effort would escape taxation if their fruits were not spent. To the extent they have any choice between consumption and savings, individuals also would gain a choice over the amount of their taxes.

Fairness has many dimensions. A particularly important dimension is what economists call vertical equity—the notion that the rich should pay more than the poor. It is often thought that because the rich tend to save more than the poor, a shift toward consumption taxation would necessarily be regressive. This need not be so, and probably would not be permitted in any legislation Congress would accept. If the choice was a consumed-income tax, it can be designed with any desired degree of progressivity just as the income tax can. A VAT or sales tax could contain a partial measure of built-in progressivity, by exempting essential items such as food and medicine, and any remaining degree of regressivity could be offset by *increasing* the degree of progressivity in the income tax. (Most discussions of a VAT or sales tax assume continuation of the income tax, possibly with some reduction in rates.) There are several features of consumption taxes that would make their ultimate effect more progressive than first appearances suggest and possibly more so than the current tax system.

First, consumption taxes are favorable to capital accumulation and growth. Increased capital accumulation presumably means higher productivity and higher wages for workers. And, as many conservatives point out, productivity and growth have done far more to improve standards of living for low-income people in the United States than all government transfer programs combined. At the same time, the law of diminishing returns implies that increases in capital supply would drive down the returns earned by the owners of capital. The Summers analyses cited above suggest that, in the long run, a shift to a consumed-income tax might raise wages by more than 15 percent and reduce pretax capital returns by more than 40 percent. Thus, an argument can be made that shifting taxes away from income and toward consumption would work largely to the long-run benefit of workers, not the owners of capital.

Second, tax shelters would be more difficult under either a consumed-income tax or a VAT. We frequently think that the important characteristic of consumption taxes is that they don't tax capital income, but consumption taxes similarly eliminate the deductions for borrowing and business losses on which most tax shelters depend. In 1979 individuals' net profits from business activities totaled $8.7 billion, and total net losses came to $11.5 billion dollars. Because consumption taxes would avoid taxing capital income, they would obviate the need for the loss allowances from which much mischief springs.

The significance of this effect is difficult to gauge. Those who are most successful in sheltering income show up in our tax statistics as poor, with very low taxable incomes, but some indirect evidence suggests that capital is increasingly escaping current taxes. The spread between municipal and taxable bond yields has narrowed greatly in recent years. Undoubtedly, this has many causes, but the current and prospective availability of methods to avoid capital income taxation must have reduced the attraction of their tax exemption for investors. No similar reduction in tax subsidies to borrowing seems to have occurred.

Third, a consumed-income tax would offer an opportunity to tax accumulated wealth, which to date has escaped taxation under the individual income tax. It would be terribly unfair to tax an individual once when income is earned, twice when it is invested, and then thrice when it is consumed. On the other hand, when income is successfully sheltered in the first place and accumulates tax-free interest, there is justice in taxing it when it is spent. A consumed-income tax would focus on encouraging new saving, but there is little to be gained by exempting consumption financed from past savings of the deceased. As a consequence, consumption taxes would offer an improved way of attacking current concentrations of wealth.

Fourth, a consumed-income tax would probably lead to some asset revaluations. (These would probably be minimized by a gradual phase-in.) In some cases, these revaluations would offset windfall gains created by the interaction of the income tax system with inflation.

Finally, consumption taxes could, in concept, reduce political objections to increasing the progressivity of the tax system. One major argument against further progressivity has been that high marginal rates interfere excessively with saving decisions. With a VAT, this argument would be weakened to the extent that the VAT revenues might be used to reduce income tax rates for lower- and middle-income taxpayers. With a consumed-income tax, the argument would not stand at all, since savings would be exempted completely from taxation. In the language of economics taxes can be more progressive if *efficiency costs* of the progressivity (for example, interference with saving decisions) can be minimized.

A standard argument of equity-oriented economists and politicians has been that consumption taxes favor the rich (since saving is not taxed and the rich do the most saving) and hurt the poor who consume their entire income. These four considerations—increased productivity and higher wages, reduced tax shelter opportunities, increased ability to tax existing wealth, and the reduced efficiency cost of progressivity—suggest that the reality is not so simple as the standard argument implies.

Overriding all the arguments pro and con for consumption taxes is a fundamental lack of empirical information to resolve the issues. Much more work is needed, first, to analyze quantitatively the economic growth arguments for and against consumption taxes and, second, to examine the experience of other countries that rely on consumption-oriented taxes. Until more systematic, quantitative, and repeatable evidence becomes available on these subjects, any movement toward consumption taxes will be vulnerable to major doubts and legitimate (or at least plausible) counterattacks.

Notes

1. Michael J. Boskin, "Taxation, Saving, and the Rate of Interest," *Journal of Political Economy*, 86 (April 1978):S3–S27.

2. Lawrence H. Summers, "The After-Tax Rate of Return Affects Private Savings," *American Economic Review*, May 1984: pp. 244–253.

3. See, for example, Boskin, "Taxation, Saving"; W.E. Weber, "The Effects of Interest Rates on Aggregate Consumption," *American Economic Review*, 60 (September 1979):591–600; C. Wright, "Savings and the Rate of Interest," in *The Taxation of Income from Capital*, ed. Arnold C. Harberger and Martin J. Bailey. (Washington, D.C.: The Brookings Institution, 1969), 275–300; E.P. Howrey and S. Hymans, "The Measurement and Determination of Loanable Funds Saving," *Brookings Papers on Economic Activity*, 3 (1978): 655–685; A.S. Blinder, "Temporary Tax Cuts and Consumer Spending," *Journal of Political Economy*, 89 (February 1981):16–53.

4. L.H. Summers, "Tax Policy, the Rate of Return and Savings," National Bureau for Economic Research Working Paper 995, September 1982; L.S. Seidman, "Taxes in a Life-cycle Growth Model with Bequests and Inheritances," *American Economic Review*, June 1983:437–442.

5. A.J. Auerbach and L. Kotlikoff, "An Examination of Empirical Tests of Social Security and Savings," National Bureau for Economic Research Working Paper 730, August 1981.

6. See, for example, L.G. Hansen and K. Singleton, "Stochastic Consumption, Risk Aversion, and the Temporal Behavior of Asset Returns," *Journal of Political Economy*, 91 (April 1983):249–265.

7. D. Runkle, "Testing for Liquidity Constraints Using Euler Equation Methods," Brown University, 1983, Mimeo; M. Shapiro, "The Permanent Income Hypothesis and the Real Interest Rate: Some Evidence from Panel Data," *Economic Letters*, 14 (1984):93–100.

8. L.H. Summers, "Capital Taxation and Accumulation in a Life-Cycle Growth Model," *American Economic Review*, 71 (September 1981): 533–544.

9. See Summers, "Tax Policy"; Shapiro, "Permanent Income Hypothesis"; Hansen and Singleton, "Stochastic Consumption."

10. Thomas Hobbes, *Leviathan*, Everyman's Library ed. (London: J.M. Dent & Sons, 1934), p. 184.

4
Simulation Methodology

Macroeconometric Models

Computer modeling became popular in economics during the 1960s and, beginning in 1968 with the development of the Data Resources, Inc., macroeconometric model of the U.S. economy, moved from being a research tool for academics into a commercial service used by hundreds of corporations and government agencies in their planning. Today, econometric modeling is a large business, and is considered a regular component of the long-range planning of many corporations. Modeling offers several benefits:

1. Since the economy is very complex with many parts interacting with one another, a model provides a convenient way for an economist to keep score of all the interactions among the various parts.
2. A model provides a discipline that helps its users to think through systematically the effects of policy changes such as a new tax on all parts of the economy.
3. Similarly, a model helps economists ensure that their assumptions about different economic phenomena are internally consistent with one another. A model helps to reveal assumptions that conflict with one another. It also helps users to recognize the multitude of assumptions that often are needed even for a seemingly simple experiment.
4. A model offers a convenient framework for incorporating new empirical information into existing theories and observing the impacts.
5. Finally, a model helps economists develop plausible scenarios and forecasts.

In recent years, models have received some bad publicity, partly as a reaction to overselling and unkept promises made during the fast-growth period of models in the 1970s as well as a reflection of new doubts about macroeconomic theories generally. Nevertheless, models retain their value as experimental tools and, properly used, can help economists to sharpen significantly their reasoning.

Various studies have shown that model-based forecasts are superior to forecasts based on intuitive judgment alone.

Types of Macromodels

There are three major types of macroeconometric models representing three different theoretical approaches to macroeconomics: income-expenditure models, monetarist models, and supply-side models.

Income-Expenditure Models. The most widely used macroeconometric models are basically descendants of the early Keynesian income-expenditure tradition, enhanced over several generations by the addition of numerous refinements such as more detailed financial sectors, the inclusion of stocks of business capital, financial wealth, and consumer durables, more rigorous treatment of the determinants of aggregate supply and prices, and more sophisticated modeling of energy linkages. These models are widely used for policy analysis and business forecasting and planning.

Monetarist Models. Monetarist models are motivated by the policy view that the most important determinant of economic activity is the money supply, which is the key (and, in many cases, only) driving policy variable. Tax rates, federal spending programs, consumer activity, and business investment incentives have only minor, if any, roles in determining aggregate economic activity. Moreover, monetarist models are usually small, with very little sectoral detail. These models are typically not as rich in federal budget and tax detail as would be necessary for our purposes.

Supply-Side Models. There has been a growing interest in supply-side economics. Generally, this term has been associated with a form of analysis that stresses the role of incentives in bringing forth greater supplies of labor, capital, and other economic factors. Although the ideas have been developed conceptually, we are aware of no purely supply-side models that have been put into commercial use. However, many of the supply-side theoretical insights have been integrated into the widely used income-expenditure models.

For our simulations, we chose the most widely used income-expenditure model, that of Data Resources, Inc. (DRI). The DRI model contains roughly one thousand equations describing activity in a large number of sectors. It contains fifteen separate consumption categories, twenty-six business investment categories, four housing categories, and thirteen categories of exports and imports. The model has a detailed *stage-of-manufacture* set of price equations that trace price changes from the raw commodity stage through wholesale prices and into final product prices. Its financial sector is the most elaborate of the commercially available models.

Example of a DRI Model Simulation

For readers who are unfamiliar with economic simulations, the following example traces through the sequence of events that occurs inside a model such as DRI when a particular change is introduced. In this example the change is a deficit-reduction program of federal spending cuts and tax increases similar to the "downpayment on the deficit" that was enacted in 1984. First, there would be a reduction in overall demand (GNP) due to the reductions in disposable income (from higher personal taxes) and reduced government spending. This will increase the unemployment rate and lower capacity utilization, putting downward pressure on both wages and prices. Depending on the stance of monetary policy, the Federal Reserve might respond to the economic weakness and ease monetary policy by providing more credit and lowering interest rates. In any case, interest rates would fall because of the softening of wages and prices, the reduced borrowing of the Treasury, and the reduced level of economic activity. If the Federal Reserve did choose to ease monetary policy, interest rates would fall further.

The lower interest rates will improve the stock market, and the combined effect on cost of capital will provide greater incentives for both corporate and private investment. Increased investment (housing as well as business investment) offsets somewhat the reduced consumption and government spending from the deficit-reduction action. Higher net investment results in a larger and more rapidly growing capital stock. The increased capital stock raises worker productivity, further reducing inflation pressures. In addition, higher productivity tends to improve standards of living and (at least temporarily) enhance international competitiveness.

This general pattern of effects is apparent in all of the tax simulations performed for this study. The specific effects and their magnitudes depend on the exact nature of the tax changes and will be discussed below.

Design of the Experiments

The modeling of alternative taxes each followed the same basic procedure. First a baseline simulation was chosen that represented the "current policy" world, namely, one that is likely to occur provided there are no major changes in economic policy or in the external economic environment.

A number of baseline scenarios were available from earlier works conducted by the DRI organization. For our purposes, the choice among these scenarios was not critical, since we were concerned with measuring only the differences caused by various tax policies. The model is essentially linear with respect to these changes, so any of a number of baseline cases would have produced equivalent results. Highlights of the baseline case we selected are summarized in table 4–1.

Table 4–1
Baseline Simulation, 1986–1991

Real GNP growth	Average of 3.1 percent/year
Inflation	Average of 5.9 percent/year
Unemployment	Edging downward to 7.0 percent by 1991
Total persons employed	Increasing about 1.4 percent/year
Productivity gains	Average of 1.5 percent/year
Wage rates	Increasing by 7 percent/year
Personal saving rate	Approximately 5 percent
Imported oil prices	Increasing 2.5 percent/year
Food prices	Declining about 1 percent/year
Monetary Policy	
Money supply growth	Average 5.5 percent/year
Short-term interest rates	Reducing from over 9 percent to 7.1 percent by 1991
Long-term interest rates	Edging downward to 10.4 percent by 1991
Government Budget	
Tax rates	Limited tax increases equivalent to a bracket creep of about 2 percent per year.
Deficits	Remaining near current levels. $153 billion in 1991, or about 2.3 percent of GNP

Starting with this baseline, each simulation introduced changes in federal tax policy, beginning in 1986, and the model was run again. The charts and tables of chapter 5 focus on the *differences* between the model's results with these changes and its results without them, that is, in the baseline case.

The time period for all analyses began in 1986, based on the assumption that any major tax reform would take sufficient time for debate and that its earliest effective date would be January of 1986. The simulations were run forward for six years through 1991 based on earlier simulation experience that indicates that six years is enough time for most effects of tax changes to fully appear, yet not so far into the future as to stretch the believability of the forecasts. It is a truism in economic forecasting that the further forecasts project into the future, the less reliable they are.

Each of the tax policy changes were designed to raise federal tax revenues by 1 percent of GNP. This choice was made to reflect the consensus of persons we interviewed in the Treasury Department and other government agencies who felt that at least some tax increases would occur in the next session of Congress in an effort to reduce the federal deficit.[1] The ways in which these additional revenues were raised depended, of course, on the particular tax being tested, as discussed below.

As with any macromodel simulation, the assumed monetary policy response of the Federal Reserve is critical in determining the economic outcomes from the tax simulations. There are several monetary policy assumptions frequently employed in simulation studies, each with different effects on the economy:

1. The Federal Reserve holds constant the growth path of banking system reserves, thus allowing the tax-induced changes in the economy to raise or lower the money supply at will. This amounts to the "default" monetary policy that would be supplied by the DRI model in the absence of some explicit choice by

the model user. While this policy is a useful research tool for certain tests, it is not a realistic assumption about actual Federal Reserve policy.

2. The Federal Reserve holds constant the growth path of the money supply, M1. This alternative assumes that the Fed has certain money-supply targets, and if the actual money supply deviates from those targets, the Fed will take action to bring the money supply back to the desired level. This is the policy the Fed has followed generally for the past decade, and it is the one we used in most of our analyses. This is often described as "nonaccomodative," meaning that, under this policy, any tax or other policy change will have a smaller effect on the economy (either negative or positive) than if reserves were held constant. For example, tax increases that tend to weaken aggregate demand in the model, will lower the demand for money and reduce the money supply below what it would have been without the change in taxes. Under a fixed money-supply policy, the Fed would ease credit conditions to offset this reduction in the money supply, thereby minimizing the negative effects of the tax increase.

3. The Fed holds constant the growth level of nominal GNP. This policy assumes that the Fed's ultimate goal is to maintain the overall state of demand in the economy. If the economy were to deviate from that path, then the Fed would "lean against the wind" and alter credit conditions enough to bring the economy (nominal GNP) back on the target path. Under this policy assumption, tax and budget policy changes would only alter the compositional mix of demand, not the overall level. This monetary policy assumption is the most "nonaccomodative," and we have presented certain tax comparisons in this context in order to highlight their differences.

4. The Fed holds short-term interest rates constant. Under this alternative, the Fed targets interest rates, not money or GNP. Stimulative tax policy or budget changes, which tend to raise interest rates, would be further enhanced by the easing of credit conditions designed to offset the increase in interest rates. Similarly, tax increases that weaken aggregate demand and thus lower interest rates would be made more contractionary by the Fed's efforts to offset the interest rate declines. This monetary policy is the most "accomodative" and was the actual policy of the Federal Reserve prior to 1970.

Of these various alternatives for monetary policy, the most plausible, given an informed assessment of the current operating stance of the Federal Reserve, was to assume that either the money supply or the level of nominal GNP was held on the baseline path.

Types of Tax Policies Simulated on the Model

Using the DRI macroeconometric model, we compared four principal taxes:

1. A conventional tax increase retaining the current tax system and raising rates enough to increase federal revenues by about $45 billion in 1986.

2. A modified flat tax (the Bradley–Gephardt proposal), which would replace the current income tax.

3. A Value-Added Tax of approximately 3.5 percent that would raise about $45 billion in 1986. The current income tax would be retained.

4. A Consumed-Income Tax that would replace the current income tax.

Each tax policy was introduced in the first quarter of 1986 and ran through the last quarter of 1991 for a total of six years.

Conventional Tax Increase

This simulation was designed as a benchmark for comparison with the other taxes in which a similar amount of tax revenue would be raised (1 percent of GNP, or roughly $45 billion at annual rates in 1986). Roughly two-thirds of the simulated tax increase would fall on individual taxpayers, and the remaining one-third on corporations. The tax increase was implemented in the DRI model by:

raising the personal tax rate by one percentage point;

raising the statutory corporate tax rate by four percentage points;

lowering the effective investment tax credit by two percentage points.

Appendix B describes the methods used to arrive at these rate changes.

A Modified Flat Tax (Bradley–Gephardt)

The second tax policy simulation implemented the Bradley–Gephardt Fair Tax Act. This proposal lowers tax rates and broadens the definition of taxable income for both individuals and corporations. According to its sponsors, Bradley–Gephardt would yield the same revenue as the current tax system in the year of its proposed implementation, 1985. However, since the tax comparisons in this report are all based on tax policies that would generate an additional 1 percent of GNP in revenues in 1986, we scaled the Bradley–Gephardt rates upward by two percentage points.

By itself, the DRI model cannot capture all the detail contained in the Bradley–Gephardt proposal. For example, the model calculates personal income taxes by multiplying a single average tax rate by a single aggregate personal tax base. Corporate tax accruals are calculated in a similar fashion. With some minor exceptions, the model does not include representation of the multiplicity of rates, exemptions, deductions, and credits that apply to individual and corporate income taxes. This is true of most macromodels and does not reflect a lack of concern for these issues, but a compromise determined by the uses to which the models are ordinarily put.

Similarly, many of the tax changes embodied in the Bradley–Gephardt proposal will have economic impacts that the model is not designed to capture. These are common obstacles in using simulation models, and the models usually provide ways for their users to introduce a variety of adjustments, so that the model will better represent the phenomena the users are trying to study. The external adjustments we introduced in testing the modified flat tax are discussed in detail in appendix B.

Value-Added Tax

The VAT is logically somewhat different from the other simulations presented here. It was designed specifically to raise revenues, and was thus an add-on to the existing system. Two of the other taxes, Bradley–Gephardt and the consumed-income tax, were both wholesale revisions to the tax code, eliminating the current income tax and replacing it with a new one.

Like the other tax proposals studied, the VAT was designed to raise federal tax revenues by 1 percent of GNP. Snce the base on which the VAT would be levied is much smaller than overall GNP, the tax rate must be higher than 1 percent. The VAT rate used in the simulations was 3.5 percent. This rate was assumed to be applied to a base of consumption expenditures that consisted of the categories listed in table 4–2.

Table 4–2
Value-Added Tax Base
(billions of dollars)

Consumption Category	1983	Percent Subject to VAT
Total	2155.9	50
Durable goods	279.8	98
Motor vehicles and parts	129.3	100
Furniture, household equipment	94.4	100
Other	46.4	86
Nondurable goods	801.7	44
Food[a] (restaurant meals and alcohol,		
are assumed to be taxed)	416.5	30
Clothing and shoes	127.0	80
Gasoline and oil	90.0	100
Fuel oil and coal	21.0	100
Other	147.2	82
Services	1,074.4	29
Housing	363.3	0
Household operation (telephone fees, gas, and		
electricity assumed to be taxed)	153.8	87
Transportation (excludes transit systems,		
and highway and bridge tolls)	72.5	93
Other (excludes medical care,		
imputations, education, and other)	484.8	25

[a]Assumed to be zero-rated.

The actual tax base amounted to 55 percent of consumption and 33 percent of overall GNP. Thus, at a 3.5-percent rate, the VAT will yield revenues equal to 1 percent of GNP. The choice of categories to exclude is arbitrary to some degree. This particular mix of taxed consumption categories corresponds with an earlier analysis of value-added taxes.[2]

As can be seen, the mix of taxable categories is predominately goods as opposed to services, and durable goods are virtually all taxed whereas many nondurable goods are not taxed.

Monetary Policy under the VAT Simulation

The selection of monetary policy is especially problematic in simulation of a value-added tax. If the Fed is assumed to rigidly hold the money supply to its previous growth rate, then the VAT's increase in prices would result in a sharp contraction in the real money supply, which would drive up interest rates and weaken the economy. Most observers feel it is more likely that the Fed would recognize that the one-time change in the price level resulting from the VAT would not, by itself, be inflationary. Rather, the Fed would focus attention on subsequent rounds of price increases that might be triggered by the VAT, and would act to limit these second-round price increases. Thus, under this assumption, the only effect on price levels would be the one-time direct effect of the VAT.

A monetary policy consistent with these goals would be one in which the Fed allowed the money supply to increase by the exact amount of the VAT's effect on overall prices (about 1 percent overall). In this way, the first-round direct effects of the VAT would not reduce the real money supply, but any subsequent increases in prices that might be triggered by the VAT would result in a lower real money supply.

In the simulations, the money supply was increased by the direct effect of the VAT (roughly 1 percent) in the first quarter of the simulation. Thereafter the money supply under the VAT simulation remained a constant 1 percent higher than the path in the baseline.

The alternative monetary policy, that of holding nominal GNP constant, also has a similar twist in the case of the VAT. For reasons that are identical to those noted above, the Fed (if it were targeting nominal GNP) would fix its new targets (after implementation of the VAT), at a level that would take into consideration the effect of the VAT on nominal GNP. Thus in those simulations, it was assumed that the Fed would allow nominal GNP to follow a path that was roughly 1 percent higher than the path in the baseline.

Consumed-Income Tax

In the case of the consumed-income tax, the entire corporate and personal tax system would be scrapped and replaced with a new system that would raise $45 billion in additional revenues. The system would retain the same basic progressivity as the current tax system.

The corporate income tax would be eliminated under a consumed-income tax. Asset purchases (equipment and structures) would be expensed, but borrowings and sales of assets would be added to income. Dividends would be a deductable expense for corporations.

We have assumed the so-called conventional treatment of home and automobile purchases. These expenditures would not be taxed at the time of purchase. But the loan repayments for these assets (both interest and principal) would not be deductible. This is equivalent (in present value terms) to taxing the entire consumption at the time of purchase and then allowing deductibility of interest and principal repayments.

Simulation Considerations

The way in which the consumed-income tax simulations were performed was conceptually different from the other tax policies. In the other policy experiments, the only "outside-the-model" adjustments that were introduced were small changes designed to capture special aspects of one tax policy or another. The Bradley–Gephardt adjustments to the housing sector and stock market were examples of these small adjustments. By contrast, the adjustments made to the model under the consumed-income tax simulation were quite extensive.

In addition to the increase in tax revenue that is common to all of the simulations, the consumed-income tax simulation also included extensive adjustments to personal consumption expenditures. Each consumption category was reduced by two percentage points below its baseline value. These adjustments to consumption were phased in over two years starting in the first quarter of 1986. Therefore, by the end of 1987, each consumption category was adjusted downward by 2 percent of its value.

Under a consumed-income tax, business capital investment outlays would be written off immediately (expensed) instead of depreciated over a number of years. This greatly reduces the cost of using business capital. The section of the model that captures the incentives for business investment was altered to capture this effect. One of the most important unanswered questions surrounding the implementation of a consumed-income tax concerns the degree to which personal saving would be increased by the higher after-tax cost of consumption relative to saving. Because of its origins as an income-expenditure model, the DRI model is not designed to measure this savings response to a consumed-income tax. Unfortunately, this was one area in which the model was unable to offer much assistance. Instead, our approach was to *assume* such an increase in savings and let the model follow the consequences from there. In other words, the approach we took toward simulating the savings aspect of the consumed-income tax was: *If* the proponents of a consumed-income tax are correct and individuals do in fact shift 2 percent of their consumption into savings, *Then*, what does the model tell us about the consequences of that shift?

The shift was phased in over a period of eight quarters to reflect the lags that probably would occur if such a tax were enacted. The level of 2 percent was chosen, somewhat arbitrarily, as being a reasonable midpoint between the effect of another consumption tax, the VAT, and the much larger assertions of some proponents of the consumed-income tax.

High-Inflation Scenario

Each of the four tax simulations was based on the same baseline forecast from DRI. In that forecast, inflation was expected to remain moderate, averaging between 5 and 6 percent annually for the remainder of the decade. To see what would happen if inflation was not so steady and moderate, we ran an alternative baseline simulation that included a higher inflation rate. Higher inflation in this alternative was introduced primarily in two ways: (1) wages were increased at a more rapid rate than in the baseline; and (2) demand conditions in raw materials markets drove up the prices of primary commodities. Other parameters of the simulation remained as in the baseline case. The high inflation scenario produced inflation rates that averaged 11 percent annually from 1986 to 1991. Over the period from 1989 to 1991 the inflation rate in the alternative baseline averaged 11.7, over five percentage points faster than the 6.2 percent inflation in the baseline case.

Several tax features were tested with this new baseline case, and their results paralleled those of the standard experiments. Variables measured in current dollar terms were larger, of course, than in the standard case, but in proportion to each other they followed almost identical patterns. For this reason the high inflation exercises were not pursued in depth.

Limitations of the Simulations

As most people recognize, a computer model, even one with a thousand equations, is at best a crude approximation of the U.S. economy. Moreover, the model is based on a set of economic theories that are themselves constantly changing as new information becomes available. Also, other modelers might choose different ways to introduce tax changes into the model than the ones we chose, or they might try different assumptions or adjustments. Thus, virtually every modeling study includes standard "warning labels" cautioning readers not to be misled by the apparent precision of computer-generated numbers and, in particular, not to fall into the trap of thinking the model has a "mind of its own" separate from the experimenter. Those warnings apply here also.

The important aspect of modeling studies is not the precision of particular forecasts or projections, rather, it is the *patterns* that are being shown. Modelers gain confidence in the patterns their models show them by running the models again and again under slightly different assumptions or using slightly different inputs each time. In the process, they develop a feel for the sensitivity of their findings to these inputs. If a particular output variable shows wide variations, that variable becomes suspect. A second way of evaluating models is to assess the plausibility of their logic. If the individual sections of the model make sense, and the model has been calibrated with accurate data, then a kind of rough justice should prevail, and the model's results will correspond generally to the way the real economy behaves.

The DRI model, with over 15 years of frequent use by hundreds of economically sophisticated customers, meets this latter test as well as any tool available to economists.

What the models lack is the precision and richness of detail that permits laboratory scientists to give absolute pronouncements and accountants to measure corporate profits down to a fraction of 1 percent. In comparison, most numbers produced by a model should be regarded as ±10 or more percent. Fortunately, the factors that make them imprecise tend to operate uniformly, so that *relative* differences and patterns tend to be reliable, though their absolute levels may be off the mark by a substantial margin. Here, again, sensitivity analyses and examination of the model's internal workings can help a user assess the validity of the results.

Time Span of Simulations

Like most such models, the DRI model is optimized for simulating business cycles a few quarters to a few years into the future. Very long-term forecasts are not only cumbersome with these models, but increasingly unreliable. Thus we limited our simulations to six years, that is, as far as 1991.

The changes brought about by major tax reforms, however, will continue to affect the economy many years into the future, and some effects, such as an increased pool of savings, will cumulate to cause even larger effects as time goes on. For these items, the model's results should be read as a *direction* and a *speed* of change, not as the final outcome. To help readers in gauging the likely degree of continued change after 1991, we have also included simulation results for 1987 and 1989 in the tables in chapter 5.

Effects of Taxes on Federal Spending

For purposes of this analysis, we have not tried to estimate the effects of different tax structures on federal spending. Yet, at least some impacts are almost certain. The present tax system contains numerous "tax expenditures" for worthy causes that may need to be replaced by direct subsidies if the tax code is changed. One example is charities. If elimination of the deduction for charitable contributions (an element in some tax simplification proposals) leads to a loss of revenues to charities, then the government may need to step in and provide (or pay for) some of the same services directly.

Notes

1. This tax increase adds realism to the simulations but methodologically it is not critical to the study's findings. Because of linearity in the DRI model, an assumption of no tax increase or of a tax increase twice as large would have produced essentially the same differences among the taxes being tested. What is important is that the simulations all be scaled for the *same* tax revenues, as they were.

2. C.E. Walker and M.A. Bloomfield, *New Directions in Federal Tax Policy for the 1980s* (Cambridge, Mass.: Ballinger Publishing Co., 1983), table 9–1, 192.

5
Simulation Findings

Each of the four tax policies used in the simulations is different in structure and implementation, but they all share two common features. First, each presupposes a federal tax increase averaging 1 percent of GNP. Second, each assumes some response by the Federal Reserve. These ground rules were enforced in all four tax simulations to ensure comparability of results. However, the ground rules introduce effects that readers should bear in mind when reading the tables and figures that follow in this chapter.

Any tax increase will reduce people's disposable incomes and hence weaken the economy. When the Federal Reserve responds, as we assumed it would, the result will be a lowering of interest rates and a stimulus to the sectors most sensitive to interest rates, particularly housing and business investment. Thus, all four tax simulations showed a common pattern of a softening of personal consumption expenditures and a relative strengthening in housing, business investment, and a few similar sectors.

In reading the tables and figures, the important aspects on which to concentrate are the *differences* among the taxes, not the effects common to all four. (A useful analogy may be the way consumer magazines often carry articles that compare different brands of television sets, refrigerators, or other products. Most of the discussion is about the differences between the products, not the features common to all brands.)

In most instances, *the common features of the simulations outweighed the differences among them.* In other words, the effects of a tax increase of this size and its ensuing Federal Reserve monetary response were more important than the particular type of tax being implemented. Such a finding may appear surprising at first, but on reflection it is easily explained.

The personal saving rate in the United States is about 5 percent. Thus, on average, peoples' incomes and consumption are identical to within 5 percent of each other. Similarly, corporate taxes fall only on profits, a small part of total revenues. Even if the current taxes were purely on income (which they are not) and were shifted to pure consumption taxes, the new taxes would cause only modest changes in macroeconomic aggregates, at least initially.

The effects of these tax changes will be subtle at first, but will cumulate over time as the nation's pool of capital builds up at a faster rate and as individuals gradually change their spending and saving habits. For this reason, we have included in the tables not only the yearly simulation results but also the cumulative differences from the baseline case over the full six-year period studied.

Gross National Product and the Unemployment Rate

These simulations were designed to be essentially neutral with respect to GNP. By imposing a monetary policy that held GNP or the money supply on its pre-existing path, any differences that the taxes caused in GNP would be purely statistical, due to such factors as rounding, slight differences in the ways the model converges to its solution, and the like. The one exception was the VAT, where nominal GNP was about 1 percent higher due to an assumed one-time expansion of the money supply.[1]

Consumption and Saving

The DRI model determines personal consumption by first calculating after-tax disposable income and then allocating that disposable income to savings (typically about 5 percent) and the different categories of consumption: nondurable goods (about 35 percent), durable goods (about 15 percent), and services (about 45 percent). The different taxes produced different levels of disposable personal income as shown in table 5-1.

The VAT and the consumed-income tax produced the largest declines in personal disposable income. Both of these taxes would fall harder on consumers than on businesses, whereas the other two taxes would split their increases proportionally between corporations and individuals.

Table 5-1
Effect of Tax Proposals on Disposable Personal Income

Tax	Disposable Income in 1991 (billions of 1983 dollars)	Six-year Cumulative Change from Baseline (percent)
Baseline case	2958.8	
Conventional Tax Increase	2899.6	-1.8
Bradley–Gephardt	2920.3	-1.6
Value-Added Tax	2893.7	-2.1
Consumed-Income Tax	2890.7	-2.2

The changes in consumption expenditures generally followed the changes in disposable income. The exception was the consumed-income tax, where a major part of the consumption outcome was dictated by the specific adjustments to consumption that were introduced into the model. Changes in disposable income are far more important (particularly within the DRI model) in determining consumption and saving outcomes than are changes in the after-tax yield on savings.

Of greater interest to us, however, were the ways in which consumers would allocate the reductions in disposable income between saving and the various categories of consumption. Table 5–2 shows this allocation for 1991, according to the simulations.

As can be seen in table 5–2, the consumption-oriented taxes did achieve their stated goal of shifting at least a small portion of consumption toward savings as compared with the conventional tax increase.[2] Somewhat surprisingly, Bradley–Gephardt did also. The primary reason for this shift is to be found in Bradley–Gephardt's elimination of consumer interest deductions.

Table 5–3 and figures 5–1 and 5–2 show in more detail the results of the four tax simulations on personal consumption and savings.[3]

Durable Goods

In all four tax alternatives, the largest relative consumption decline was in durable goods, where the average declines ranged between 2 percent and 4 percent by 1991. This was almost twice the overall decline in consumption expenditures. Several factors caused this pattern. First, durable consumption is always the most volatile and responsive to changes in disposable personal income. Second, a Value-Added Tax would fall disproportionately on durable goods. As discussed in chapter 4, 98 percent of durable goods expenditures would be taxed under the assumed value-added tax versus 55 percent for nondurables and 29 percent for services. Finally, in the case of the Bradley–Gephardt tax, removal of the deductibility of consumer interest would increase the after-tax cost of borrowing to pay for these big-ticket items and would reduce durable goods consumption below what it would otherwise be.

Table 5–2
Allocation of Disposable Personal Income in 1991
(in percent)

	Nondurables	Durables	Services	Savings	Other	Total
Baseline case	32.8	13.9	45.7	4.8	2.8	100
Conventional tax increase	33.1	13.8	46.3	4.0	2.8	100
Bradley-Gephardt	32.8	13.8	46.0	4.6	2.8	100
Value-Added Tax	33.0	13.6	46.4	4.2	2.8	100
Consumed-Income Tax	32.4	13.7	45.5	5.6	2.8	100

Table 5-3
Personal Consumption Expenditures and Saving Rate

	1987	1989	1991	Cumulative
Consumption expenditures (billions of 1983 dollars)				
Baseline value	2457.3	2598.0	2734.3	
Difference from baseline (percent)				
Conventional tax increase	-0.9	-1.1	-1.2	-1.0
Bradley-Gephardt	-1.3	-1.2	-1.0	-1.1
Value-Added Tax	-1.4	-1.5	-1.6	-1.5
Consumed-Income Tax	-2.8	-3.3	-3.1	-2.9
Durable goods consumption (billions of 1983 dollars)				
Baseline value	344.8	377.1	407.2	
Difference from baseline (percent)				
Conventional tax increase	-1.9	-2.1	-2.5	-2.0
Bradley-Gephardt	-2.7	-2.2	-1.7	-2.1
Value-Added Tax	-3.6	-3.7	-4.1	-3.8
Consumed-Income Tax	-3.8	-4.0	-3.5	-3.6
Nondurable goods consumption (billions of 1983 dollars)				
Baseline value	901.1	934.2	967.8	
Difference from baseline (percent)				
Conventional tax increase	-0.8	-1.0	-1.2	-0.9
Bradley-Gephardt	-1.1	-1.2	-1.3	-1.1
Value-Added Tax	-1.0	-1.3	-1.5	-1.2
Consumed-Income Tax	-2.6	-3.2	-3.4	-2.8
Service consumption (billions of 1983 dollars)				
Baseline value	1205.4	1278.0	1348.4	
Difference from baseline (percent)				
Conventional tax increase	-0.7	-0.8	-0.8	-0.7
Bradley-Gephardt	-1.0	-0.9	-0.5	-0.8
Value-Added Tax	-0.9	-0.8	-0.8	-0.8
Consumed-Income Tax	-2.7	-3.0	-2.7	-2.6
Personal saving rate (percent of disposable income)				
Baseline value	5.0	4.9	4.8	
Difference from baseline (absolute)				
Conventional tax increase	-0.6	-0.8	-0.8	-4.3
Bradley-Gephardt	-0.6	-0.5	-0.2	-2.8
Value-Added Tax	-0.5	-0.6	-0.6	-3.5
Consumed-Income Tax	0.6	0.8	0.8	3.8

Note: Monetary policy assumption: money supply held on baseline path.

One factor influencing durable goods consumption, particularly in the later years of the simulation, was the increase in housing activity that was a common feature in all four tax simulations. (This increase will be discussed below in the section on residential construction.) The increase in housing starts and sales tended to result in larger outlays for certain categories of consumer durables (furniture, appliances, furnishings, and so forth).

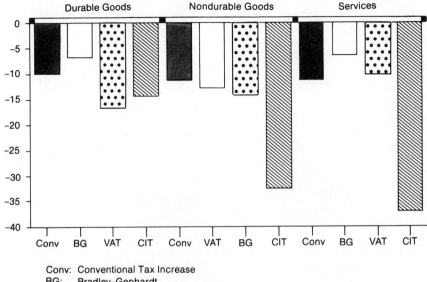

Conv: Conventional Tax Increase
BG: Bradley–Gephardt
VAT: Value-Added Tax
CIT: Consumed-Income Tax

Figure 5-1. Constant-Dollar Personal Consumption Expenditures in 1991 (difference from baseline simulation, billions of 1983 dollars)

Other Categories of Consumption

The changes in nondurable and service consumption were relatively slight in all of the tax alternatives except the consumed-income tax, where the assumed reduction in consumption expenditures was a major factor in the outcomes shown in table 5-3.

The saving rate fell in all except the consumed-income tax simulation. In that simulation, the assumed adjustment to consumption outlays resulted in increases in the personal saving rate. In all of the other tax alternatives, the decline in savings due to the tax increase was larger than the gain in saving due to the changes in tax structure.[4]

Residential Construction

Table 5-4 and figure 5-3 show the effect of the tax changes on residential construction. As discussed at the beginning of this chapter, residential construction was stronger in all four of the tax alternatives than in the baseline simulation. By 1991, the increase ranged from about 4 percent (under the conventional tax increase and the value-added tax) to about 9 percent (under Bradley–Gephardt).

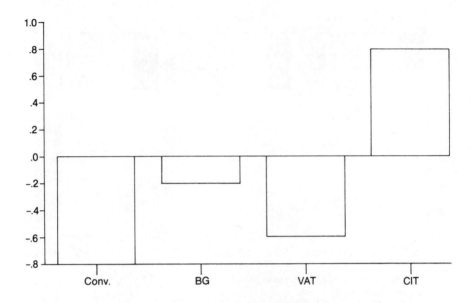

Figure 5-2. Personal Saving Rate in 1991 as Percentage of Disposable Personal Income (difference from baseline simulation, percentage points)

The counter-intuitive Bradley–Gephardt outcome deserves an explanation. Recall that as part of the implementation of Bradley–Gephardt, single- and multiple-family housing starts were reduced to capture the fact that mortgage interest and real estate taxes could only be deducted against income in the lowest tax bracket. This reduction in the value of these deductions increased the after-tax cost of housing. The actual outcome, as can be seen in table 5–4, was that total housing starts were higher under Bradley–Gephardt than under the baseline. (The increase in single-family starts more than offset the decline in multiple-family starts.) This occurred because the reductions in interest rates that resulted from the monetary stimulus outweighed the Bradley–Gephardt adjustments to the housing equations.

The decline in multiple-family starts under Bradley–Gephardt and the consumed-income tax resulted from a combination of lower interest rates, which tends to make home ownership more attractive than renting, and the reduced advantage of real estate depreciation under these alternative tax systems.

Business Investment

Table 5-5 shows the effects of the four tax alternatives on business investment spending. All the tax alternatives other than the conventional tax increase

Table 5-4
Residential Construction

	1987	*1989*	*1991*	*Cumulative*
Residential construction (billions of 1983 dollars)				
Baseline value	157.2	164.6	164.3	
Difference from baseline (percent)				
Conventional tax increase	3.3	4.5	4.2	3.7
Bradley–Gephardt	1.4	5.5	6.1	3.7
Value-Added Tax	8.9	7.0	6.3	6.8
Consumed-Income Tax	5.3	10.7	16.0	9.2
Total private housing starts (millions of units)				
Baseline value	1.819	1.818	1.720	
Difference from baseline (absolute)				
Conventional tax increase	0.078	0.096	0.078	0.454
Bradley–Gephardt	0.014	0.089	0.090	0.260
Value-Added Tax	0.197	0.141	0.117	0.819
Consumed-Income Tax	0.117	0.202	0.344	1.066
Single-family private housing starts (millions of units)				
Baseline value	1.144	1.150	1.096	
Difference from baseline (absolute)				
Conventional tax increase	0.074	0.089	0.071	0.421
Bradley–Gephardt	0.063	0.133	0.134	0.540
Value-Added Tax	0.186	0.130	0.107	0.763
Consumed-Income Tax	0.160	0.236	0.373	1.293
Multiple-family housing starts (millions of units)				
Baseline value	0.674	0.668	0.624	
Difference from baseline (absolute)				
Conventional tax increase	0.005	0.007	0.007	0.034
Bradley–Gephardt	−0.048	−0.044	−0.044	−0.279
Value-Added Tax	0.012	0.010	0.009	0.056
Consumed-Income Tax	−0.042	−0.035	−0.029	−0.227

Note: Monetary policy assumption: money supply held on baseline path.

raised the business investment share of GNP. Figure 5–4 depicts the same information, graphically and highlights the impact of a consumed-income tax on business investment. The outcomes shown in table 5–5 are, for many economists, the primary goal of tax reform. To understand the relative impacts of these four tax alternatives on business investment, it is helpful to inspect what each does to the desirability of investment.

Within the DRI model, actual investment results are determined by specific business investment incentives such as accelerated depreciation. A conventional tax increase would hurt investment incentives by reducing the investment tax credit and raising corporate tax rates, thus increasing the cost of capital to businesses, especially for equipment purchases (which benefit from investment tax credits). As can be seen, the reduced investment expenditures in this simulation were largely due to declines in equipment investment.

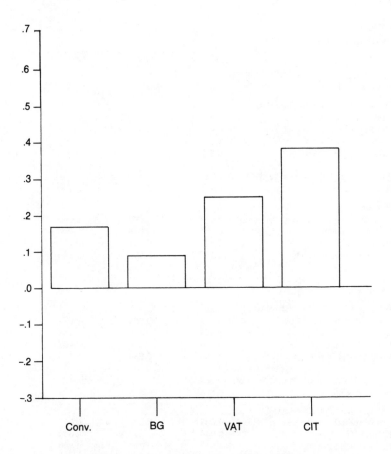

Figure 5-3. Residential Construction in 1991 as Percentage of Gross National Product (difference from baseline simulation, percentage points)

The tax changes embodied in Bradley–Gephardt pull investment incentives in opposite directions. On the one hand, the elimination of investment tax credits and the scaling back of depreciation allowances from what is allowed under current tax law will reduce the desirability of investments. On the other hand, the reduction of the top corporate tax rate from 46 percent to 30 percent (or 32 percent in this simulation), increases the attractiveness of investments. In the simulations, the latter effect was the stronger of the two, so that on balance total business investment was greater than in the baseline. However, the *type* of business investment changed, with equipment purchases being reduced and investment in structures being increased.

Table 5–5
Business Fixed Investment

	1987	1989	1991	Cumulative
Producers' durable equipment investment (billions of 1983 dollars)				
Baseline value	296.7	323.7	349.7	
Difference from baseline (percent)				
Conventional tax increase	-0.9	-1.3	-1.1	-1.0
Bradley–Gephardt	-0.4	-0.4	0.0	-0.3
Value-Added Tax	-0.5	0.7	1.6	0.5
Consumed-Income Tax	-0.9	0.0	0.8	-0.1
Nonresidential structures investment (billions of 1983 dollars)				
Baseline value	164.2	178.6	190.8	
Difference from baseline (percent)				
Conventional tax increase	-1.0	-0.9	-0.5	-0.8
Bradley–Gephardt	1.4	2.5	3.7	2.2
Value-Added Tax	0.2	1.1	1.7	0.9
Consumed-Income Tax	5.6	8.3	10.3	7.2
Business fixed investment (percent of GNP)				
Baseline value	12.0	12.3	12.6	
Difference from baseline (absolute)				
Conventional tax increase	-0.1	-0.1	-0.1	-0.4
Bradley–Gephardt	0.1	0.2	0.3	1.1
Value-Added Tax	-0.1	0.0	0.2	0.1
Consumed-Income Tax	0.3	0.5	0.6	2.4
Stock of business equipment (billions of 1983 dollars)				
Baseline value	1499.5	1659.7	1823.2	
Difference from baseline (percent)				
Conventional tax increase	-0.1	-0.5	-0.7	-0.4
Bradley–Gephardt	-0.1	-0.2	-0.2	-0.1
Value-Added Tax	-0.1	0.0	0.4	0.1
Consumed-Income Tax	-0.2	-0.2	0.0	-0.1
Stock of business structures (billions of 1983 dollars)				
Baseline value	1920.6	2044.0	2178.7	
Difference from baseline (percent)				
Conventional tax increase	-0.1	-0.2	-0.3	-0.2
Bradley–Gephardt	0.1	0.4	0.9	0.4
Value-Added Tax	0.0	0.1	0.3	0.1
Consumed-Income Tax	0.3	1.5	2.8	1.3

Note: Monetary policy assumption: money supply held on baseline path.

The consumed-income tax provided a large boost to investment outlays, primarily because this type of tax would allow full expensing of business investments. This immediate write-off of investments greatly reduces the effective cost of capital to business and thus provides a strong investment incentive.

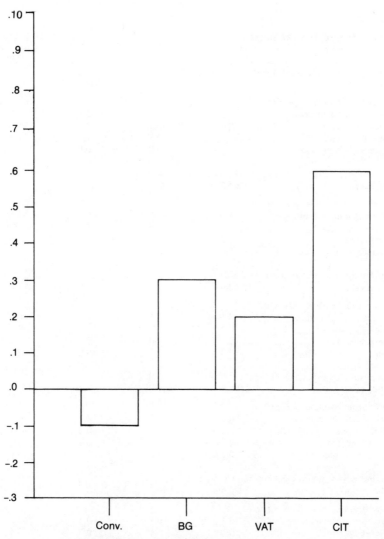

Figure 5-4. Business Fixed Investment in 1991 as Percentage of Gross National Product (difference from baseline simulation, percentage points)

While these improvements in the investment picture tend to support the position of economists who favor consumption taxes, a word of caution is in order. *The most important factors causing investment growth were specific investment incentives* embedded in the tax proposals, for example, a lower corporate tax rate or the expensing of investments, not the fact of a larger capital pool per se. The larger capital pool played a supporting role by helping to hold down interest rates, but the specific incentive provisions accounted for most of the impacts.

Foreign Trade

Table 5–6 and figure 5–5 show the effects of the four tax alternatives on exports and imports.

The key factor affecting the foreign sector was the decline in the value of the dollar. This decline ranged from about 1 percent under the conventional tax increase to as much as 6 percent under other alternatives. Declines in the exchange rate can be traced to the declines in interest rate levels. The conventional tax increase showed smaller reductions in interest rates than the three tax proposals and therefore showed a smaller decline in the dollar.

The foreign sector contained another effect that in some respects had more significance for this study than the direct effects of foreign trade. In all four simulations, foreign investment increased, primarily because of the exchange rate and reduced U.S. interest rates. This subject will be taken up in a later section.

Table 5–6
Exports and Imports

	1987	*1989*	*1991*	*Cumulative*
Exports (billions of 1983 dollars)				
Baseline value	422.2	474.3	533.2	
Difference from baseline (percent)				
Conventional tax increase	0.1	0.5	0.7	0.4
Bradley–Gephardt	0.2	1.4	2.8	1.3
Value-Added Tax	0.6	1.7	2.0	1.3
Consumed-Income Tax	0.3	1.5	2.2	1.2
Imports (billions of 1983 dollars)				
Baseline value	496.1	532.0	570.0	
Difference from baseline (percent)				
Conventional tax increase	−1.1	−1.7	−2.0	−1.4
Bradley–Gephardt	−1.3	−2.2	−3.0	−2.0
Value-Added Tax	−1.8	−2.3	−2.5	−2.0
Consumed-Income Tax	−2.4	−3.5	−3.6	−2.9
Net exports (billions of 1983 dollars)				
Baseline value	−73.9	−57.8	−36.9	
Difference from baseline (absolute)				
Conventional tax increase	5.8	11.5	15.2	57.3
Bradley–Gephardt	7.6	18.5	32.2	98.5
Value-Added Tax	11.3	20.1	24.9	100.1
Consumed-Income Tax	12.9	25.6	32.6	124.9
Multilateral exchange rate (June 1970 = 1.0)				
Baseline value	0.92	0.89	0.87	
Difference from baseline (percent)				
Conventional tax increase	−0.8	−1.5	−1.4	−1.1
Bradley–Gephardt	−1.6	−3.9	−6.2	−3.3
Value-Added Tax	−2.5	−3.7	−4.0	−3.1
Consumed-Income Tax	−2.3	−3.7	−4.7	−3.1

Note: Monetary policy assumption: money supply held on baseline path.

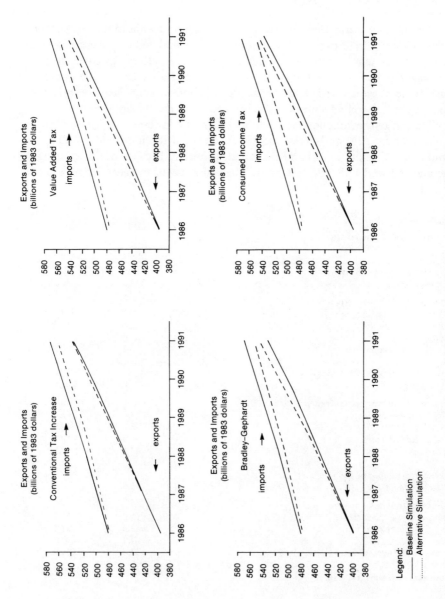

Figure 5-5. Growth in Exports and Imports under Alternative Tax Proposals

Prices and Wages

Table 5–7 shows the effects of the four tax alternatives on prices and wages.

The most significant change in wages and prices was, as expected, the VAT-induced price increases. The other simulations showed relatively slight decreases in overall prices. In general, the slight economic weakness that resulted from the tax increases was reflected as a slight softening in prices.

The differences in inflation rates between these simulations and the baseline, except for the VAT's one-time change, were almost imperceptible (less than 0.1 percent per year on average).

Wage changes tended to follow price changes. The taxes with the largest effects on output and prices (particularly the consumed-income tax) also had the largest effects on compensation rates. Real wages were down slightly under the

Table 5–7
Prices and Wages

	1987	1989	1991	Cumulative
Implicit price deflator for GNP (1983 = 1.0)				
Baseline value	2.603	2.919	3.291	
Difference from baseline (percent)				
Conventional tax increase	−0.1	−0.3	−0.5	−0.3
Bradley–Gephardt	0.0	−0.3	−0.3	−0.2
Value-Added Tax	1.0	1.0	0.9	1.0
Consumed-Income Tax	−0.1	−0.5	−1.0	−0.5
Implicit price deflator for consumption (1983 = 1.0)				
Baseline value	2.563	2.868	3.232	
Difference from baseline (percent)				
Conventional tax increase	−0.1	−0.3	−0.5	−0.2
Bradley–Gephardt	0.0	−0.3	−0.3	−0.2
Value-Added Tax	1.6	1.6	1.5	1.6
Consumed-Income Tax	−0.2	−0.7	−1.1	−0.6
Consumer price index (1967 = 1.0)				
Baseline value	3.650	4.101	4.648	
Difference from baseline (percent)				
Conventional tax increase	−0.1	−0.3	−0.5	−0.3
Bradley–Gephardt	0.0	−0.2	−0.2	−0.1
Value-Added Tax	1.7	1.7	1.6	1.7
Consumed-Income Tax	−0.2	−0.7	−1.2	−0.6
Hourly compensation (nonfarm business sector, 1977 = 1.0)				
Baseline value	2.070	2.401	2.814	
Difference from baseline (percent)				
Conventional tax increase	−0.2	−0.5	−0.9	−0.5
Bradley–Gephardt	0.0	−0.3	−0.3	−0.2
Value-Added Tax	0.4	0.8	0.9	0.7
Consumed-Income Tax	−0.5	−1.3	−2.1	−1.2

Note: Monetary policy assumption: money supply held on baseline path.

conventional tax increase and the consumed-income tax due to the economic weakness, unchanged under Bradley–Gephardt, and down slightly under the value-added tax due to a less-than-complete catch-up of wages to the higher prices of consumer items.

The Federal Budget

The federal revenues and deficits produced by these simulations were not properly *outcomes* of the study, since they were direct consequences of the tax programs fed into the model. Nevertheless, it is instructive to look at the results, depicted in table 5–8 to gain a few insights into the functioning of tax programs once they are installed.

After starting with approximately equal revenues, the four taxes drifted apart over the next several years both in revenues and in government expenditures. They would have drifted even further apart if we had not introduced a correction into the Bradley–Gephardt tax. As proposed, Bradley–Gephardt would remove indexing from the individual tax system. Thus, inflation would once again tend to drive individuals into higher tax brackets year by year. This bracket creep, although less strong than occurred with the unindexed current

Table 5–8
Federal Expenditures, Revenues, and Deficit

	1987	1989	1991	Cumulative
Federal expenditures (billions of dollars)				
Baseline value	1121.1	1316.4	1544.5	
Difference from baseline (absolute)				
Conventional tax increase	−8.3	−23.4	−37.8	−118.1
Bradley–Gephardt	−10.3	−32.6	−52.7	−162.1
Value-Added Tax	−8.7	−22.8	−34.1	−110.2
Consumed-Income Tax	−16.6	−46.3	−77.8	−238.0
Federal revenues (billions of dollars)				
Baseline value	930.4	1145.6	1391.0	
Difference from baseline (absolute)				
Conventional tax increase	37.4	40.2	43.4	240.2
Bradley–Gephardt	33.0	42.0	47.2	241.8
Value-Added Tax	38.7	46.8	53.7	275.3
Consumed-Income Tax	38.5	40.4	48.3	254.1
Surplus or deficit (−)				
Baseline value	−190.7	−170.8	−153.4	
Difference from baseline (absolute)				
Conventional tax increase	45.7	63.7	81.1	358.3
Bradley–Gephardt	43.4	74.7	99.9	404.0
Value-Added Tax	47.4	69.7	87.7	385.5
Consumed-Income Tax	55.1	86.7	126.1	492.1

Note: Monetary policy assumption: money supply held on baseline path.

system in the 1970s, was still significant and would produce more and more tax revenue each year. In the simulations, we removed that influence, as if Congress legislated periodic tax cuts to offset the bracket-creep. This was done to maintain consistency of the tax alternatives for comparison purposes.

Bradley–Gephardt contained another hidden revenue raiser that also needed to be offset in the simulation to maintain rough consistency with the other taxes. Because people's incomes would be expanded to include health insurance benefits, the Bradley–Gephardt proposal would add these amounts to the Social Security tax base, thereby increasing the Social Security taxes of both employees and their employers.

The reduction in federal expenditures shown in table 5–8 was due entirely to reduced costs for debt service. (We assumed no changes in other government programs.) Debt service costs were reduced in two ways. First, the added tax revenues reduced the amount of deficits below the baseline projection and thus saved some interest costs. Second, since the taxes (and the resulting Federal Reserve reaction) caused interest rates to fall, the government's cost for already outstanding debt was reduced.

National Saving

Table 5–9 shows the effects on overall national saving rates from the four tax alternatives. Figures 5–6, 5–7, 5–8, and 5–9 depict the simulation results graphically for each of the four tax alternatives. All four taxes produced sizeable increases in national saving. The greatest change was under the consumed-income tax, which increased national saving by roughly 10 percent. The next largest increase in national saving was caused by the VAT; the conventional tax increase caused the smallest increase.

The increase in saving came from two offsetting sources. First, private saving (the sum of personal and business saving) was reduced in all of the tax alternatives. Disposable personal incomes and corporate after-tax retained earnings were all reduced as a result of the tax increases, and this reduced private saving. Offsetting these private declines in saving was a sharp increase in government saving, reflecting the added federal revenues being used to reduce deficits. This increase obviously resulted from the significant reductions in the federal deficit under the four alternatives.

The consumed-income tax caused the greatest increase in public saving and the smallest decline in private saving, because, of all the taxes, it added the greatest amount to the total pool of savings. Thus its gain in national saving was roughly 50 percent greater than any of the other tax alternatives; it was about eight times greater than the national saving increase under the conventional tax simulation.

Table 5-9
Aggregate Saving and Investment
(billions of dollars)

	1987	1989	1991	Cumulative
Total saving	663.8	823.7	1003.6	(baseline)
Difference from baseline				
Conventional tax increase	2.7	8.5	13.5	43.4
Bradley–Gephardt	8.1	30.9	59.9	161.6
Value-Added Tax	22.9	41.6	58.9	215.9
Consumed-Income Tax	25.2	62.9	100.7	318.7
Private saving	791.1	920.0	1074.6	(baseline)
Difference from baseline				
Conventional tax increase	−39.1	−50.7	−61.0	−287.2
Bradley–Gephardt	−22.4	−33.7	−27.1	−174.3
Value-Added Tax	−17.5	−20.9	−17.7	−121.3
Consumed-Income Tax	−19.5	−13.3	−10.9	−109.3
Personal saving	159.4	184.0	214.2	(baseline)
Difference from baseline				
Conventional tax increase	−22.4	−32.0	−38.1	−176.0
Bradley–Gephardt	−21.2	−21.3	−13.1	−116.5
Value-Added Tax	−17.7	−25.1	−27.3	−134.7
Consumed-Income Tax	16.3	23.8	27.8	111.4
Corporate saving	631.8	736.0	860.4	(baseline)
Difference from baseline				
Conventional tax increase	−16.7	−18.6	−22.9	−111.2
Bradley–Gephardt	−1.2	−12.4	−13.9	−57.8
Value-Added Tax	0.2	4.2	9.5	13.4
Consumed-Income Tax	−35.8	−37.1	−38.7	−220.7
Government saving	−127.4	−96.4	−71.0	(baseline)
Difference from baseline				
Conventional tax increase	41.7	59.1	74.5	330.6
Bradley–Gephardt	30.4	64.6	86.9	335.8
Value-Added Tax	40.4	62.5	76.6	337.2
Consumed-Income Tax	44.6	76.2	111.6	428.0
Business fixed investment	552.6	679.8	830.9	(baseline)
Difference from baseline				
Conventional tax increase	−5.9	−10.4	−12.5	−50.3
Bradley–Gephardt	2.9	8.0	21.1	49.3
Value-Added Tax	−1.0	7.9	17.7	39.9
Consumed-Income Tax	7.0	15.9	26.3	81.7
Residential investment	193.9	232.9	268.7	(baseline)
Difference from baseline				
Conventional tax increase	6.1	9.2	9.0	43.3
Bradley–Gephardt	3.0	12.7	17.3	53.8
Value-Added Tax	16.9	16.0	16.8	88.6
Consumed-Income Tax	9.5	21.9	37.6	114.3

Table 5–9 continued

Foreign investment	−126.3	−136.1	−148.2	(baseline)
Difference from baseline				
Conventional tax increase	5.0	10.5	18.3	57.5
Bradley–Gephardt	5.5	9.8	17.4	55.4
Value-Added Tax	8.0	15.9	23.1	83.5
Consumed-Income Tax	13.2	26.5	35.2	131.4

Note: Monetary policy assumption: money supply held on baseline path.

Not all of the increased saving became domestic investment, and not all of the domestic investment went to businesses. First, foreign investment increased (or foreign disinvestment decreased) due to the lower exchange rate. This change was greatest for the tax alternative causing the largest reduction in interest rates, namely, the consumed-income tax. Over one-third of its improvement in national saving went to foreign investment. Approximately another one-third of the total went to residential housing investment. *Thus, only about one-quarter of the increased savings went to business fixed investment, the primary economic goal of tax reform.*

The value-added tax and the Bradley–Gephardt tax alternatives produced smaller increases in national saving than the consumed-income tax. Nevertheless, the changed patterns of saving were significant under both of these alternatives. The value-added tax provided a somewhat larger increase in net foreign investment, primarily due to the change in the nominal value of net exports. The savings gains produced by the value-added tax were somewhat exaggerated in

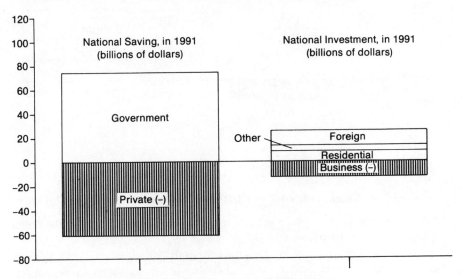

Figure 5–6. Conventional Tax Increase (difference from baseline simulation)

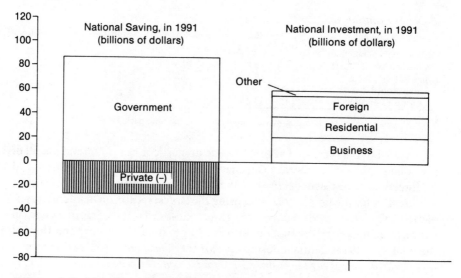

Figure 5-7. Bradley–Gephardt Tax (difference from baseline simulation)

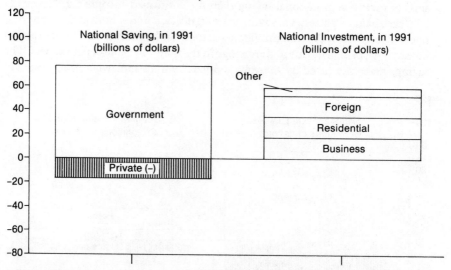

Figure 5-8. Value-Added Tax (difference from baseline simulation)

table 5-9 by the VAT's price level increases, which swelled the nominal dollar amounts by about 1 percent.

The conventional tax increase was the only tax alternative that did not increase business investment. Under that alternative, the increased saving was exhausted by the increases in residential construction and in net foreign investment.

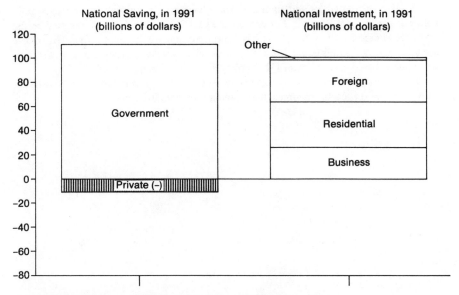

Figure 5-9. Consumed-Income Tax (difference from baseline simulation)

Notes

1. As a purely technical matter, the results for GNP and unemployment did show modest variations across taxes in the simulation that assumed a constant money supply policy by the Federal Reserve. These differences occurred because of an interesting economic phenomenon known as the velocity of money, that is, the rate at which money circulates (as opposed to sitting idle) in different sectors of the economy. Aggregate velocity in an economy is equal to GNP divided by the money supply.

Not surprisingly, velocity tends to be highest in the business sectors and slowest in the household sector. Thus, any tax that shifts consumption into savings will tend to increase velocity and, under a constant money supply policy, will result in a higher GNP than taxes that do not induce such a shift.

A second factor affecting velocity is interest rates. Obviously, the higher rates are, the greater will be the incentives for businesses and households to put idle cash balances to work. Thus, any taxes that tend to push down interest rates, as the consumed-income tax would do, will reduce velocity and thereby depress GNP somewhat under a constant money supply policy.

2. According to the DRI organization, the savings rate in the baseline case is too low because of particular parameters used in this simulation. To be consistent with recent savings rates, the figure should be adjusted upward by several tenths of a percentage point. Similarly, the figure shown for "Other," which is mostly interest payments, is about two-tenths of a percentage point higher than in normal experience. These adjustments, however, will not affect the differences among tax simulations.

3. Most of the tables and figures in this chapter reflect a constant money supply policy of the Federal Reserve. For certain analyses, a constant GNP policy may be the preferred choice, for example, where it is desired to compare the taxes with the size of the economy held absolutely equal. For readers who wish to make such comparisons, a second set of tables based on a constant GNP policy is included in appendix C.

4. This pattern would change over time. As consumers became accustomed to living within smaller disposable incomes, their saving rate would rise again.

6
Summary and Conclusions

In the early chapters of this book we emphasized that, despite the large number of tax reform proposals, these proposals cluster around two basic goals and, consequently, two basic approaches toward changing the federal tax system.

1. Stimulating economic growth through greater capital formation. The tax reforms most often associated with this goal are consumption taxes such as a VAT or a consumed-income tax. (While some consumption tax advocates argue that such taxes would be simpler and more fair than the current system, these considerations are secondary to their basic goal of growth.)
2. Improving public confidence in the fairness and workability of the federal tax system. The tax reforms most associated with this goal are tax simplification (broadening the tax base) and a flatter rate structure.

Overlying both of these approaches and their proposed reforms is a widespread concern that federal taxes will need to be increased in the near future, and that a return to the rates of the 1970s will be politically unacceptable.

Tax Reforms for Economic Growth

The basic chain of logic for using the tax system to encourage economic growth is as follows:

1. Shift taxes from income toward consumption, thereby exempting savings and most income from capital.
2. This will raise after-tax yields and increase the supply of savings and consumption will decline.

3. A larger national pool of savings (and the monetary stimulus that would follow a decline in consumption) will substantially reduce interest rates and other costs of capital.

4. Businesses, facing a lower cost of capital, will invest more in plant and equipment.

5. New plant and equipment will increase the productivity of American workers and improve competitiveness of American industries abroad, leading to a stronger economy and rising standards of living.

This logic is very appealing, but our simulations show two important weak links in the chain of reasoning. First, little empirical evidence is available to support the presumed increase in saving. In fact, as discussed in chapter 3, conventional wisdom holds there would be very little increase. The fragmentary evidence presented in chapter 3 still does not offer any practical guides for estimating the magnitude of the response, and so in our consumed-income tax simulation, we were forced to simply postulate that this savings response would occur and then follow through the economic effects.

Second, even assuming that the tax changes did induce savings, our simulations indicated that the benefits of such a reform would be diluted in major ways. *More than 70 percent of any increase in national savings brought forth by the tax would be claimed by foreign investment, residential construction, and similar adjustments to the changed economic environment.*

The implication of such a major dilution of economic impact is this: If a major goal of tax reform is to stimulate business investment, then the best course is to focus attention on specific incentives to stimulate the types of investment desired. Taking the indirect route of spurring savings to produce a larger capital pool is likely to be much less effective.

Many people may view an expansion of the housing market, or a reduced reliance on foreign capital, as desirable ends in their own right. But these are not the benefits normally promised by advocates of consumption taxes. Rather, their principal aim is to stimulate business investment, thus raising productivity and U.S. international competitiveness.

The principal flaw in the reasoning for consumption taxes, as outlined above, is in its failure to take into account the other sectors of the economy that are sensitive to interest rates. Both residential housing and business structures investment are strongly sensitive to interest rates, and any significant reduction in rates would lead to increased construction. Similarly, because of its high real interest rates, the United States now receives more than $100 billion annually of investment capital from foreigners. A reduction in rates, while it would help U.S. exports, would cause a significant reduction or runoff of this foreign capital—enough, in these simulations, to consume more than one-third of any new savings induced by a change to consumption taxes.

Other sectors sensitive to interest rates, but with much smaller overall impact, are inventory investment and infrastructure investment, such as roads, bridges, and schools.

Thus, as appealing as the logic outlined above may be, it oversimplifies the operation of an enormously diverse and complex economy, so that in the end, only about one-quarter of the induced savings (assuming it occurs) would find its way into the purposes for which the consumption taxes were installed.

A related conclusion is that the *tax system has limited power to affect the economy, at least within the types of tax alternatives and the ranges of rates considered in this book.* By far the largest factor affecting the economy in our simulations was the *size* of a tax increase and not the particular *form* in which the money was raised. Similarly, the greatest effects on net national saving were the reductions of government *dissaving* rather than any increases in private saving. Thus, much of the choice among tax alternatives will probably center around political leanings, public opinion, and ease of administration rather than their specific effects on the economy. (The overall *level* of taxes is, of course, a different question.)

The quantitative analyses used in our study indicate that the postulated economic benefits from a move to consumption taxes would be real but much smaller than first appearances suggest. The strongest shifts are associated with the tax considered most difficult politically to enact and the most difficult to implement, the consumed-income tax. Those who wish to improve U.S. international competitiveness will find that the tax system can make a small contribution in that direction, but will by no means be sufficient in itself to accomplish that goal. Moreover, the results in proportion to the costs and difficulties of a major change in federal tax collection practices are likely to prove disappointing.

Combination Approaches

The federal tax system serves several important social and economic functions:

1. Raising the funds needed to finance the government.
2. Redistributing income.
3. Providing a measure of relief for persons affected by such hardships as the blindness, disabilities, and major casualty losses.
4. Promoting basic social values relating to family, home ownership, charity, and retirement security.
5. Encouraging certain desired forms of economic activity, for example, oil and mineral exploration, rehabilitation of historic buildings, and development of alternative energy sources.

6. Helping to maintain citizens' trust in the sensibility and fairness of government.

7. (Proposed) Promoting saving and investment to spur economic growth.

The challenge before the nation is to accommodate a stepped-up demand for revenues and at the same time make progress toward goals 6 and 7 above, which are receiving increased attention. There are many who argue that these added goals are simply too much to accomplish within the structure of an income tax alone. That is, the income tax will be unable to shoulder so many responsibilities. Thus, one major argument in favor of a VAT or national sales tax is that it would provide a "third leg for the stool," the other two being the income tax and the Social Security payroll tax. Adding a third basic type of tax obviously would give the government more combinations and options to use in trying to meet these multiple (and occasionally conflicting) goals. But like any major change, this move would carry its own drawbacks, for example, a small measure of inflation, a possible temptation toward greater government spending, and the costs of administering and collecting a new type of tax.

Combination approaches using a consumed-income tax are also conceivable, and one approach may be simply to expand the limits for IRAs in the current tax system. However, neither the advocates of tax simplification nor those proposing consumption taxes appear to have embraced such a concept, probably because it would be only a partial measure and would still carry the disadvantages inherent in the current system.

Appendix A
Brief Sketch of the DRI Model

In the DRI model, GNP is determined by adding up the elements of aggregate demand (consumption, investment, government purchases, and so forth). Consumption is a function of disposable income, wealth, interest rates, and relative prices. Investment is divided into three parts: business investment, housing investment, and inventory investment. Business fixed investment depends on real output, the capacity utilization rate, the existing stock of business capital, and tax and interest rate factors. Housing investment depends on demographic factors, mortgage finance, personal income, and interest rates. Inventory investment depends on final sales, "surprises" in final sales, and interest rates. Exports and imports depend on foreign and domestic demands, respectively, and on relative prices. Government demands consist of exogenous federal purchases plus endogenous state and local purchases that depend on income, the age-distribution of the population, and interest rates.

The demand for labor is derived from the level of aggregate demand in the economy and the nature of the function governing the production of aggregate output. Thus GNP, derived by adding up final demands, together with the average productivity of the work force, determine total employment. This labor demand determines the unemployment rate depending on labor supply. Together with price expectations the unemployment rate determines the rate of wage inflation.

Average unit labor costs derived from worker compensation and productivity together with selected measures of economic slack (capacity utilization, the gap between full-employment GNP and actual GNP, and so forth) and exogenous energy and raw material prices determine the overall prices of final demands. These together with the real demands determine nominal GNP. The key differences between this approach and that of the monetarist models is thus apparent. In monetarist models nominal GNP is determined in a single equation driven by money-supply growth rates.

Nominal GNP, determined by the product of real demands and prices, is then allocated on the income side. The major charges against income are depreciation, indirect business taxes, corporate profits, rent, interest, and compensation.

The settings of various tax parameters and government spending functions is clearly important in this allocation process. These incomes provide the driving forces behind the real demands thus closing the commodity-demand-to-income loop.

The financial sector is linked with real demands through interest rates. Short-term interest rates are calculated from money demand and supply relationships. Monetary policy has its chief effects on short-term interest rates in this sector of the model.

Table A–1 summarizes the key equations and relationships in the DRI model.

The model includes single equations for each of four major categories of taxation: personal, corporate, indirect business, and social insurance contributions. Personal taxes are calculated by multiplying a single effective personal tax rate by the personal income tax base. This effective personal tax rate depends on the level of household incomes and the changes in federal tax policy.

Table A–1
Brief Overview of the DRI Macromodel

Category	Key Determinants
Major categories of real (constant-dollar) final demand	
Consumption	disposable income, prices, interest rates, household wealth.
Business investment	interest rates, capacity utilization, capital stock, corporate cash flow, stock market.
Housing investment	disposable income, mortgage interest rates, availability of mortgage finance, home prices.
Real GNP	the sum of consumption, investment, government purchases, net exports.
Labor markets and prices	
Labor demand	real GNP, wage rates, capital stock.
Labor supply	unemployment rate, tax rates, demographics.
Unemployment rate	labor demand and supply.
Wage rates	unemployment rates, prices, taxes (Social Security and UI taxes, and so forth).
Prices	wages, capacity utilization, raw material prices, unemployment rate, indirect taxes.
Current-dollar GNP	the product of real demands and final-demand prices.
Incomes	
Labor compensation	wage rates, labor demand (hours or persons).
Profits	national income less labor compensation and other categories of income.
Disposable income	compensation, entitlement benefits, personal income taxes.
Fiscal and monetary policy	
Taxes	tax rates and incomes (wages, adjusted gross income, corporate profits, and so forth).
Spending	policy assumptions concerning expenditure and benefit levels, demographics, unemployment rates, inflation.
Interest rates	real GNP, prices, Federal Reserve policy, loan demand, price expectations.

Corporate taxes are similarly determined by multiplying an effective corporate tax rate by book profits. In addition, the effect on corporate tax liabilities of the investment tax credit and the research and development tax credits are explicitly modeled.

As incomes rise or fall, the tax bases for these two categories also rise and fall. In addition, in the case of personal taxes, as the income tax base rises and falls, the effective tax rate will also rise and fall reflecting the progressivity of the individual income tax system.

Appendix B
Implementation of
Tax Simulations

S imulation studies using complex models such as the DRI model, require a host of specific assumptions concerning such things as starting conditions, monetary policy, and the mechanisms by which the simulated tax changes will first be felt by the U.S. economy. This appendix describes the technical adjustments that were made to the DRI model to implement the four tax alternatives.

Conventional Tax Increase

This simulation is designed to be used as a benchmark for comparison with other simulations in which a similar amount of tax revenue is raised (1 percent of GNP, or roughly $40–$45 billion at annual rates in 1986). Roughly two-thirds of the simulated tax increase falls on personal taxpayers, the remaining one-third falls on corporations. The tax increase was implemented in the DRI model by:

> raising the personal tax rate (RTPGF) by 0.0096 in every quarter of the simulation;

> raising the statutory corporate tax rate (RTCGFS) by 0.04 in every quarter;

> lowering the effective investment tax credit (RITC) by 0.02 in every quarter.

The ex-ante effects of these changes are shown in table B–1.

The Fair Tax Act of 1983—Bradley-Gephardt

The second tax policy simulation implements the Bradley-Gephardt (BG), Fair Tax Act. This proposal lowers tax rates and broadens the definition of

Table B-1
Increases in Personal and Corporate Income Taxes[a]
(differences from the baseline simulation, billions of dollars)

	1986	1987	1988	1989	1990	1991
Personal Taxes						
Increase rate	28.1	30.6	33.3	36.2	39.4	42.9
Corporate Taxes						
Increase rate 4 percent	9.4	10.9	11.8	12.4	13.2	14.1
Lower ITC by 2 percent	6.2	6.9	7.7	8.4	9.2	10.2
Total corporate	15.6	17.8	19.5	20.8	22.4	24.3
Total	43.7	48.4	52.8	57.0	61.8	67.2

[a]Ex-ante increases. Actual change in personal and corporate taxes will differ due to the changed state of the economy.

taxable income at both the individual and corporate level. (A more complete description can be found in chapter 2.) According to its sponsors, BG would yield the same revenue as the current tax system in the year of its proposed implementation, 1985. However, the tax comparisons in this report are all based on tax policies that generate an additional 1 percent of GNP in revenues in 1986. While recognizing that BG is designed to be "revenue-neutral," we assume here that the overwhelming pressure to reduce the federal deficit will result in a slight increase in the BG tax rates in order to raise the additional revenue. In this way it can be compared on an equal footing with the other tax policies. According to congressional estimates, an increase in the BG base and surtax rates of one percentage point would yield $23 billion in 1985. Accordingly, in the simulations, the three BG personal tax rates were assumed to be two percentage points higher than proposed.

By itself, the DRI macroeconometric model cannot capture all of the detail contained in the BG proposal. For example, the model calculates personal income taxes by multiplying a single average tax rate by a single aggregate personal tax base. At the corporate level, corporate tax accruals are calculated in a similar fashion. With some minor exceptions, the model includes no representation of the multiplicity of rates, exemptions, deductions, and credits that apply to individual and corporate incomes. This is true of most macromodels and reflects not a lack of concern for these issues, but a compromise determined in large part by the uses to which the model is ordinarily put.

Many of the tax changes embodied in the BG proposal will have economic impacts that the model is not designed to capture. Because of this, numerous adjustments had to be made to the model on the basis of primarily outside-the-model calculations and assumptions. This section details the most significant of those adjustments.

Mortgage Interest and Property Taxes

Under BG, there would be three tax rates set at 14 percent, 26 percent, and 30 percent. The last dollar of income would be taxed at the highest of the surtax rates that was applicable based on a taxpayers income. However, those few deductions that are retained under BG are used to offset income in the lowest bracket, not the highest as under current law. Thus a taxpayer in the 30 percent tax bracket would deduct mortgage interest and property taxes at 14 percent rather than 30 percent.

This feature of the proposal, which is designed to equalize the benefits of each dollar of deductions across taxpayers, would dramatically reduce the value of deductions to taxpayers whose marginal tax rates are in the upper two brackets. One result would be an increase in the cost of owner-occupied housing. Mortgage interest payments and real estate taxes will, on an after-tax basis, become more costly to the typical taxpayer claiming these deductions.

The housing sector of the DRI model does not contain a way to capture this increased cost of owner-occupied housing. But it cannot be ignored in an analysis of the BG proposal. To get around this limitation, several adjustments were made to the housing sector of the model.

To calculate the consequences of the proposed change, one needs to know the marginal tax rate of the typical taxpayer currently claiming home mortgage interest and compare it to what it would be under BG. The comparison also requires specification of the way in which tax rates affect the cost of owner-occupied housing.

Current Marginal Tax Rate. The Statistics of Income (SOI) for 1981 were investigated to estimate the current marginal tax rate of the typical taxpayer claiming deductions. Table B-2 summarizes the required calculations.

The table presents data on income and tax rates for those returns claiming itemized deductions. The first column shows the average adjusted gross income (AGI) for those returns in each of the twelve AGI classes. The second column shows the average deduction on each return (net of the zero bracket amount). The third shows the average number of exemptions per return in each of the AGI classes. With this data on average number of exemptions and average deductions in each class, it is possible to estimate an average taxable income for each of the AGI classes. This is shown in column four. The taxable income is here defined as AGI less deductions less the number of exemptions multiplied by $1,000. As can be seen, the table indicates that the average taxable income of returns with AGI falling between $30,000 and $50,000 is $29,922. The fifth column shows the tax rates that would apply to those taxable incomes (assuming the tax rates of married joint-return filers). The final column shows the distribution of total home-mortgage interest deductions by those AGI classes. The marginal tax rate

Table B-2
Income and Tax Rates of Returns Claiming Itemized Deductions
(*dollars unless otherwise noted*)

Adjusted Gross Income	Average AGI per Return	Average Deduction per Return	Average Exemptions per Return	Estimated Taxable Income	Tax Rate (percent)	Percentage of Home Mortgage Deductions
Under $5,000	2,980	0	1.5	1,461	0	0.6
$5,000 under $10,000	7,806	1,535	2.0	4,243	11	2.5
$10,000 under $15,000	12,639	1,952	2.3	8,420	15	5.4
$15,000 under $20,000	17,662	2,178	2.6	12,901	17	8.5
$20,000 under $25,000	22,557	2,632	2.9	17,069	19	11.8
$25,000 under $30,000	27,471	3,134	3.1	21,226	23	13.6
$30,000 under $50,000	37,971	4,763	3.3	29,922	30	37.6
$50,000 under $100,000	63,841	10,200	3.4	50,265	40	15.8
$100,000 under $200,000	131,204	25,259	3.5	102,438	48	3.3
$200,000 under $500,000	281,824	59,242	3.5	219,096	50	0.9
$500,000 under $1,000,000	665,223	162,644	3.3	499,230	50	0.1
$1,000,000 or more	2,104,318	566,894	3.3	1,534,130	50	0.1

Source: Internal Revenue Service, *Statistics of Income*, 1983.

of those deducting home-mortgage interest is simply a weighted average of the tax rates in column five, where the weights are the percents in column six.

The marginal tax rate of those claiming home-mortgage interest deductions is calculated to be 27.6 percent in 1981. Using estimates of the increase in personal income between 1981 and 1985, table B-2 can be "blown up" to derive estimated AGI, deductions, and taxable income and income tax rates for 1985. Based on these adjustments, the marginal tax rate of those claiming home-mortgage interest deductions in 1985 is roughly 30 percent.

Under BG the marginal tax rate (for mortgage deductions) would fall from 30 percent to 14 percent. (Under the BG variant simulated here, which raises additional federal revenues, the tax rate for deductions would be 16 percent.) The value of the deductions for both mortgage interest and property taxes would fall substantially due to the reduction in tax rates that apply to these deductions.

The most common way of capturing the impact of tax rates on housing demand is through a measure referred to as the user cost of housing.[1] A simplified version of that measure is

$$C = [(1 - t)i - q + d + (1 - t)tp] \, ,$$

where C equals the annual user cost of owner-occupied housing, as a percent of the purchase price of the home, t equals the personal income tax rate, i equals the mortgage interest rate, q equals the expected increase in the relative price of houses, d equals the house depreciation rate, and tp equals the property tax rate.

This relationship was used to estimate the change in the user cost of housing that would occur under BG. The results show that for a reduction in the tax rate, t, from 30 percent to 16 percent, the user cost of housing would increase by 20 percent.

Since the housing sector of the DRI model does not have a fully articulated measure of the user cost of housing, we were forced to adopt somewhat ad-hoc procedures to capture the impact on housing of the reduction in tax rates. The key housing equations in the DRI model are those for single- and multiple-family housing starts. Both of these are determined (in the model) by the mortgage interest rate, but not by income and property tax rates. Thus in these equations, the mortgage rate can be thought of as the variable that, in a rough-and-ready way, captures the user cost related factors influencing housing. The procedure followed here was to adjust the housing equations downward by an amount consistent with a certain increase in the mortgage interest rate. Applying the estimated 20 percent increase in the user cost of housing to the mortgage rate was too much because the mortgage rate captures other factors besides the user cost. For instance, it is a measure of the pretax hurdle costs facing first-time home buyers. This measure of housing affordability would not change under BG. Home buyers would still have to qualify for loans based on average mortgage principal and interest payments.

We lacked any formal means of determining the exact effect that a 20 percent increase in the user cost of housing ought to have on mortgage rates within DRI's housing sector. The final decision was to adjust the housing equations by the amount consistent with a 10 percent increase in mortgage rates. (Note that it would not have been correct to actually adjust the mortgage rates directly because elsewhere in the model, deposit flows and portfolio adjustments are determined, in part, by the difference between mortgage rates and other interest rates. If we had adjusted mortgage rates to capture this user cost effect then those yield differentials would have been incorrect.) The actual change in housing starts is listed in table B–3.

These changes were introduced as adjustments to the individual equations. The actual outcomes for housing starts will depend on these adjustments as well as all of the other factors that influence the equations.

The Stock Market

A key element of the BG proposal is to do away with the special treatment of capital gains income. The DRI model does not explicitly include capital gains rates but, as in the housing example, there is a general sense that changes in the tax treatment of capital gains would have an effect on the economy, particularly the stock market. The stock market is a critical variable within the DRI model, influencing the value of household wealth and therefore consumption decisions as well as the cost of financial capital for businesses and therefore investment decisions. Thus it is important to capture the impact on the stock market of changing the tax treatment of capital gains.

Estimating the change in the stock market is an extremely difficult and uncertain process. There were two independent estimates of the effect on the stock market of the changed capital gains treatment. The first considers the likely extra taxes that would be paid on capital gains in the future under BG. These additional taxes are then "capitalized" in the value of the stock market by taking its discounted present value. The present value of the additional taxes to be paid on capital gains is then deducted from the value of the stock market.

A second approach relies on a simple model of the stock market that considers the expected value of a stock, including its likely after-tax dividend stream over a relevant holding period, and the expected value of the after-capital-gains-tax proceeds from selling the stock at the end of the holding period. With

Table B–3
Effect of Conventional Tax Increase on Housing Starts

	1986	1987	1988	1989	1990	1991
Single family	−0.078	−0.094	−0.094	−0.094	−0.094	−0.094
Multiple family	−0.056	−0.056	−0.056	−0.056	−0.056	−0.056
Total	−0.134	−0.150	−0.150	−0.150	−0.150	−0.150

this simple model it is possible to analyze changes in the tax treatment of both capital gains taxes and taxes on ordinary income. This was the approach followed by Brinner and Brooks.[2]

Capitalizing the Additional Taxes.   Table B–4 summarizes recent Treasury information on capital gains realized and capital gains taxes paid.

As can be seen, the most recent three years of data show taxes on capital gains to be running around $12 billion per year. According to data from a 1978 Treasury study of capital gains by asset type in 1973, capital gains (net of losses) on financial assets (stocks and bonds) accounted for roughly 30 percent of all capital gains. If this were the case in 1981, then capital gains on corporate stocks might have been around $4 billion. The effective tax rate for that year is 15.4 percent (12.4 divided by 80.9). Assuming under BG that the marginal tax rate on capital gains would have been 28 percent, then the capital gains taxes would have been around $4 billion higher. If this annual rate of higher taxes (in real 1981 dollars) were to continue indefinitely, and assuming that the real rate of discount in the stock market is 6 percent, then the capitalized value of these additional taxes would equal $67 billion (4 divided by 0.06). In 1981 the total market value of equity held by individuals and corporations was $1,643 billion. Reducing this by the value of the additional taxes on capital gains amounts to a 4 percent reduction.

Expected Value of Stock Holding.   The simple stock market model that was used by Brinner and Brooks is not meant to be a complete representation of stock prices but a measure of the expected present value of holding the stock in a risk-free environment. It captures the value of the expected dividend stream (after tax) over the stock's holding period as well as the expected proceeds from the sale of the stock at the end of the holding period. The relevant values are discounted by an after-tax rate.

Using this model it is possible to calculate the change in the present value index that would result from the two critical features of the BG tax proposal: (1) the reduction in the dividend taxes, and (2) an increase in the capital gains tax rate. Note that the first of these, the reduction in the tax rate on dividends and other income will increase the value of the stock market by raising the after-tax value of the dividend stream from the stock. In addition, a tax rate reduction will also raise the after-tax discount rate. This will reduce the importance of capital

Table B–4
Capital Gains and Taxes
(billions of dollars)

	1976	1977	1978	1979	1980	1981
Total capital gains	39.5	45.3	50.5	73.4	74.6	80.9
Taxes	6.6	8.1	9.3	11.7	12.5	12.4

gains in determining the overall yield from stock holding particularly for longer holding periods.

Using the Brinner–Brooks model and applying reasonable parameter estimates taken from their article, it was estimated that BG would reduce the value of the stock market by about 4 percent, the same as the alternative procedure described above. Thus the stock market index in the DRI model was reduced by 4 percent to capture the effect of changed tax rates on dividend income and capital gains.

Consumer Credit Effects

The only allowed personal interest deductions under BG are for home mortgages. Thus the after-tax interest costs of other borrowings would increase. In particular, car loans and other forms of consumer finance would be more costly. The one channel for this influence in the consumption sector of the DRI model is through a variable capturing the operating costs of an automobile, JCOST-CAR. This captures several factors including the interest rate on consumer borrowing. It was estimated that going from a tax system in which consumer interest is deductible to one in which it is not would result roughly in a 20 percent increase in the effective after-tax interest cost of those borrowings. This, in turn, would produce a 4 percent increase in the variable JCOSTCAR, given the structure of its equation. Therefore, the JCOSTCAR equation was adjusted upward by 4 percent.

Municipal Bond Interest

BG would greatly reduce the amount of municipal bond interest that could be excluded from income for tax purposes. Interest on borrowings other than general obligation bonds would no longer be excluded from income. The two biggest kinds of borrowing that this would effect are industrial revenue bonds (IRBs) and mortgage subsidy bonds (MSBs). The interest cost to state and local governments from issuing debt for these purposes would be much higher. However, within the DRI model, the only spending category that is affected by the municipal bond rate is state and local construction funded by general obligation bonds. These borrowings would remain tax free and thus not be affected by the BG proposals. Therefore no change was made in the municipal bond interest rate even though it is clear that it would have to rise by an amount that would equalize the risk-adjusted rates on IRBs and MSBs with competing assets.

Health Insurance Costs

Another feature of BG is that employer-paid medical and dental insurance would be counted as income for tax purposes. These compensation benefits would no longer be tax free. The effect of these changes is to increase the cost of medical insurance both to the employee and to the employer. The employee's cost is now higher because taxes must be paid on these benefits. The employer's cost is higher because the value of these benefits would be counted in the Social Security tax base and thus raise the employer's social insurance contributions.

Because of the increased costs of medical insurance, individuals would have a greater incentive to limit coverage by purchasing plans with higher deductible amounts. In addition, people would reduce their overall demand for health care services. It is difficult to estimate the exact magnitude of these changes on the distribution of health care and of national resources. In any case, the DRI model is not well suited to capture these influences. One aspect of the change, however, can be handled within the model. It is likely that the very rapid increase in medical service costs would be reduced slightly by these changes. To capture this effect, the increase in medical care costs was assumed to average 1 percent per year less than it would have under the current tax treatment of medical insurance benefits. In the DRI model, consumer medical costs are included in the prices of *Other Services*. The price deflator for *Other Services* was reduced by 0.4 percent per year from what it would have been as a result BG.

In addition, social insurance contributions were raised by an amount designed to capture the additional taxes to be paid on these benefits. The exclusion of employer group life insurance and accident and health insurance from income would cost the federal government roughly $30 billion in 1986 according to tax expenditure estimates from the Office of Management and Budget and from the Congressional Budget Office. Assuming an average tax rate of around 25 percent, this implies benefits totaling around $120 billion. Assuming that 85 percent of this amount or about $100 billion would be added to the taxable wage base (some of these benefits go to people not in the Social Security system and to those whose incomes exceed the maximum taxable wage base). With a combined employer-employee tax rate of 14.3 percent, this additional income in the wage base will yield $14 billion in 1986. The effective social insurance contribution rate in the DRI model (RTWGF) was increased by enough to account for this change.

Changes in Corporation Taxes

To capture the corporate tax changes proposed by BG, the statutory corporate tax rate was lowered to 30 percent and the investment tax credit and the research and development tax credit rates were set to zero. In addition, the effective economic lives and tax depreciation rates were changed to capture the effect of the change to an alternative depreciation scheme from the present Accelerated Cost Recovery System (ACRS).

Structures

Under ACRS, business structures are depreciated over 15 years (actually 16 years, when the half-year convention for the first year is taken into account). The amount of depreciation that can be claimed in each year is based on tables from the Treasury Department. It depends on the month in which the structure was placed in service.

Under BG, business structures will have an "infinite life" and a declining-balance depreciation rate that is based on economic lifetimes. Based on analysis from the Commerce Department's Bureau of Economic Analysis, it was assumed that the average economic life for structures is approximately thirty years. BG provides for depreciation based on a 250% declining-balance method. The actual rate would be 250% of the straight-line depreciation amounts. Thus for a 30-year asset the depreciation rate for structures under BG would be 0.0833 (2.5 divided by 30). In addition, the half-year convention will continue to apply under BG. This means that in the first year of service, only one-half of the value of an asset is eligible for depreciation.

Table B–5 compares the amount of depreciation that can be claimed in each year under BG with that of the current tax system (ACRS).

The variables within the DRI model that determine the allowed tax depreciation (DELTAIPDENRs) were set equal to the amounts shown in the BG column of table B–5.

After 16 years, structures are completely depreciated under ACRS but only about 75 percent depreciated under BG. Thus the present value of the depreciation allowances is clearly lower under BG. This is one of the key factors in the way that the model determines the desirability of investment expenditures. Reduced depreciation allowances lower the desirability of investment from two sources: (1) they lower the after-tax cash flow of the firm, and (2) they tend to

Table B–5
Annual Depreciation Amounts for Business Structures
(in percent)

Year	ACRS	BG	Difference (ACRS – BG)
1	6.5	4.2	2.3
2	10.9	8.0	2.9
3	9.7	7.3	2.4
4	8.5	6.7	1.8
5	7.5	6.2	1.3
6	6.5	5.6	0.9
7	6.0	5.2	0.8
8	5.9	4.7	1.2
9	5.7	4.3	1.3
10	5.3	4.0	1.3
11	5.0	3.6	1.4
12	5.0	3.3	1.7
13	5.0	3.1	1.9
14	5.0	2.8	2.2
15	5.0	2.6	2.4
16	2.4	2.4	0.1
Amount of depreciation remaining after 16 years	0	26.0	

increase the after-tax cost of the purchased capital. What matters in this regard is the present value of the depreciation allowances.

Table B–6 shows the present value of depreciation allowances (PVD) under the two systems for alternative discount rates. The difference between the PVD under ACRS and BG varies with the discount rate, but generally it is in the neighborhood of 0.10 to 0.12.

The present value of the tax depreciation amounts is not the only factor affecting the desirability of business investment. Other important factors include the effective interest rate that a firm must pay for its funds, and the tax rate that must be paid on the income generated by the asset. In addition, the investment tax credit provides incentives for investing in equipment by lowering the after-tax cost of the asset. Finally, the rate at which the income generated by the asset is taxed—the corporation tax rate—is also an important factor in determining the desirability of investment.

All these factors are combined in what is referred to as the *rental price* of structures or equipment investment. This measures the effective rental price that a firm would have to charge itself over the life of the asset to pay for the use of the investment good. If the depreciation allowance is scaled back (as it would be under BG), then the firm would have to charge itself more for using the capital if it were to just break even. Alternatively, if the corporation tax rate were lowered (as it would be under BG), then the firm could charge itself less rent from the use of the capital asset.

The familiar formula for determining the rental price is

$$c = \frac{P \star [(d + r) \star (1 - t \star PVD + ITC)]}{(1 - t)},$$

where P is the relative price of equipment or structures, c is the rental price, d is the economic depreciation rate (the rate at which the physical capital decays), r is the cost of financial capital, t is the corporate tax rate, PVD is the present value of depreciation allowances (on a scale of 0 to 1.0), ITC is the investment tax credit, which is equal to zero for structures.[3]

Table B–6
Present Value of Depreciation Allowances per Dollar of Investment (alternative discount rates)

Discount Rate (percent)	ACRS	BG	Difference (ACRS − BG)
10	0.599	0.477	0.122
12	0.553	0.434	0.119
15	0.496	0.384	0.113
17	0.465	0.357	0.108
20	0.425	0.324	0.102

The rental price of structures under ACRS is 0.872 and under BG, 0.792, assuming the state and local government effective corporate tax rate is equal to 9 percent and the relative price of structures equals 3 (an estimate of its value in 1986 when the proposal is scheduled to take effect.

As can be seen, the introduction of BG will cause the rental price of structures to fall due to the decline in the corporate tax rate, which is large enough to offset the deterioration in the value of depreciation allowances.

Equipment

Unlike structures, the rental price of equipment would increase under BG due to the proposed elimination of the ITC. This factor, combined with the reduction in depreciation allowances, is powerful enough to outweigh the positive effects of the decline in the corporate tax rate.

Under ACRS, equipment falls under either three-year or five-year depreciation schedules. Depreciation allowances per dollar of investment are shown in table B–7. A weighted average of the two equipment classes is shown in the third column of the table. If the ITC is claimed on equipment investment, then the basis for depreciation is reduced by one-half of the ITC amount. Thus in figuring depreciation allowances (assuming that equipment purchasers will claim the ITC), these amounts are reduced by 5 percent. The adjusted depreciation amounts are shown in the fourth column. Finally the table shows the depreciation amounts that would be allowed over the first five years for equipment under BG. It was assumed that equipment would have a ten-year average life.

The PVD under ACRS and BG depreciation for alternative discount rates are shown in table B–8.

In a fashion similar to that of structures, the rental price of equipment can be calculated, with the only important difference being the inclusion of the ITC. Using a representative cost of financial capital of 13 percent, the rental price of equipment under ACRS would be 0.581 and would increase under BG to 0.662.

Table B–7
Equipment Depreciation Allowances under ACRS and BG
(per dollar of investment)

Year	Three Year	Five Year	Equipment Average	After Adjustment	BG
1	0.25	0.15	0.169	0.161	0.125
2	0.38	0.22	0.230	0.219	0.219
3	0.37	0.21	0.222	0.211	0.164
4		0.21	0.194	0.184	0.123
5		0.21	0.185	0.176	0.092
Amount remaining after 5 years					0.276

Table B-8
Present Value of Depreciation Allowances per Dollar of Investment (alternative discount rates)

Discount Rate (percent)	ACRS	BG	Difference (ACRS - BG)
10	79.3	75.0	4.3
12	76.8	71.6	5.1
14	74.4	68.6	5.8
16	72.2	65.9	6.3
18	70.1	63.4	6.7
20	68.1	61.1	7.0

Other Changes

Many state income tax systems "piggy-back" on the federal tax system, using the federal tax definition of adjusted gross income as their tax bases. States with these kinds of plans would, if nothing happened to offset it, receive an enormous windfall under BG. Taxpayers would have to declare much higher (25 percent) income, but there would not have been a corresponding reduction in state income taxes. Thus taxes would be higher by roughly 25 percent in these states. It was assumed that this was not a desired result from BG and the effective state and local individual tax rate was lowered to offset the increase in the income tax base, leaving overall state and local tax revenues at a level consistent with what they would have been without the implementation of BG.

Simulation of BG

The changes noted above were introduced into the baseline simulation to produce a changed economy based on the BG proposals. This new simulation resulted in changes in both the money supply and in nominal GNP as compared with the baseline. Monetary policy was then adjusted by increasing or decreasing nonborrowed reserves of the federal reserve system in such a way as to produce (1) the same path for the narrow money supply as was in the baseline simulation, and (2) the same path for nominal GNP as was in the baseline simulation. These simulations are described in detail in chapter 4.

Value-Added Tax

As discussed in chapter 4, the VAT is logically somewhat different from the other simulations presented here, being an add-on to the current tax rather than a replacement of it.

Like the other tax proposals studied here, the VAT is designed to raise federal tax revenues by 1 percent of GNP. The VAT rate used in the simulations was 3.5 percent. This was assumed to be applied to a consumption tax base that consisted of the categories of consumption listed in table B–9.

The VAT was implemented in the model by increasing all of the final prices in the model by an amount consistent with the fraction of each consumption category that is taxed at 3.5 percent. For instance, the consumption of motor vehicles and parts is fully taxed at 3.5 percent. Thus the price for this category of consumption is raised by 3.5 percent. By contrast, a large fraction of food consumption will be untaxed. In that case the price of food is only raised by 1.3 percent (0.36 times 3.5 percent).

In addition to the prices of consumption goods, the prices of several other categories of GNP were also changed. The VAT would require that all intermediate products, except those that are zero-rated, would bare the full 3.5 percent of the VAT. Thus in the model implementation of the VAT, wholesale prices (except farm prices) were increased by 3.5 percent.

Table B–9
Value-Added Tax Base
(billions of dollars)

Consumption Category	1983	Percent Subject to VAT
Total	2155.9	45
Durable goods	279.8	98
Motor vehicles and parts	129.3	100
Furniture and household equipment	94.4	100
Other[a]	46.4	86
Nondurable goods	801.7	44
Food[b]	416.5	36
Clothing and shoes	127.0	0
Gasoline and oil	90.0	100
Fuel oil and coal	21.0	100
Other[c]	147.2	99
Services	1,074.4	29
Housing	363.3	0
Household operation[d]	153.8	87
Transportation[e]	72.5	93
Other[f]	484.8	25

Note: Consumption (percent of GNP): 65.2
      VAT base (percent of GNP): 29.6

[a]14 percent of "Other" includes ophthalmic products and orthopedic devices that were assumed to be untaxed.

[b]Assumed to be zero-rated. Restaurant meals and alcohol are assumed to be taxed.

[c]Excludes net foreign remittances.

[d]Telephone fees, gas, and electricity assumed to be taxed.

[e]Excludes transit systems, and highway and bridge tolls.

[f]Excludes medical care, imputations, education, and other.

Import prices were increased to reflect the levying of the tax on all (nonfood) imported goods. Exports prices were adjusted to insure that they were unaffected by the VAT. In the DRI model, the prices of exports are based on the prices of similar domestically traded goods. Since the prices of these domestically traded goods would increase due to the VAT, the model wants export prices to increase as well. Export prices had to be adjusted to maintain their no-VAT levels.

The prices of homes and of new home construction were not changed, reflecting the assumption that housing would be exempt from the VAT. This is an area of some disagreement. Alternative assumptions about the VAT treatment of housing would necessarily yield somewhat different results.

Monetary Policy under the VAT Simulation

As discussed in chapter 4, the selection of monetary policy in simulating a value-added tax requires a choice between two basic assumptions: (1) that the Federal Reserve would take a "hard line" stance on money supply, making no special accommodation to the VAT, or (2) that the Fed would permit a one-time expansion in money supply to accommodate the VAT, but would act to limit any second-round price increases that might be triggered by the imposition of the VAT.

In these simulations, we chose the second assumption as being more likely. The money supply was increased by the direct effect of the VAT (roughly 1 percent) in the first quarter of the simulation and thereafter remained a constant 1 percent higher than the path in the baseline. Similarly, in simulating the alternative monetary policy, that of holding nominal GNP constant, it was assumed that the Fed would allow nominal GNP to follow a path that was roughly 1 percent higher than the path in the baseline.

Consumed-Income Tax

The implementation of the consumed-income tax presented a more difficult set of problems than the other tax proposals. Like Bradley–Gephardt, it would replace the entire existing tax system, but unlike Bradley–Gephardt, it would not require integrating the corporate and individual income tax systems, something the models are not currently designed to do. In addition, the proponents of the consumed-income tax expect their policy to have effects on personal saving behavior. These beliefs are based on assumptions about how individuals respond to changes in the after-tax yields on savings. The current structure of the DRI model is not well suited for answering questions about the kinds of consumption changes that would occur following a change in the taxation of consumption versus saving.

Moreover, at a purely practical level, introducing a consumed-income tax into a model structured in a fashion similar to DRI's model poses a host of other problems. Under most variants of the consumed-income tax, individuals would establish qualifying accounts for deposits of income that would be untaxed. In addition, they would have to declare any net borrowing since this amount would also be included in the tax base. Thus the income tax base under a consumed-income tax would be very different from the current one. As a modeling exercise, to estimate the effects of a consumed-income tax on tax receipts and disposable income, we would have to know the value of net borrowings. This is not a variable within the DRI model. And even if it were, it is not now coded to be included in the tax base for personal taxes.

There are a similar set of problems in modeling tax receipts at the corporate level. First, it may be that, as under many variants of the consumed-income tax, corporations are taxed on the basis of their cash flow. Cash flow would be defined to include not only the traditional measures (retained earnings plus the depreciation allowances) but also net borrowings. The DRI model is not currently designed to handle this.

Under other variants of the consumed-income tax, corporations would completely escape tax and pass their effective net income down to the individual shareholders. This form of integration would pose additional modeling problems.

The upshot of all of this is that the DRI model was not used to test the effects of a particular sort of consumed-income tax. Instead, the model was used in a somewhat different fashion. The baseline simulation was changed in such a way as to increase federal revenues by 1 percent of GNP. The way in which this was done was similar to the first simulation described above, namely, the increase in taxes from "conventional" sources. In addition, each consumption category was reduced from its baseline value two percentage points. (These adjustments to consumption were phased in over two years so that by the fourth quarter of 1987, each consumption category was adjusted downward by 2 percent of its value.) It should be noted that these changes were entered as adjustments to the equations, and not to the actual values of each consumption category. The actual change in consumption in the simulation depends on a great many factors, this adjustment included.

One common feature of all consumed-income tax proposals is the treatment of business investment outlays. Investment outlays would be expensed or deducted immediately in the period in which the purchase was made. Thus the present value of the depreciation allowances under a consumed-income tax proposal would be exactly equal to one. To accurately model the adjustment process away from consumption to investment that would be induced by the consumed-income tax, it was necessary to insure that the essential elements of corporate investment decisions were modeled accurately.

The monetary policy assumptions were similar to those described above. In one the money supply was held at its path in the baseline simulation, in the other nominal GNP was held at its base path.

High-Inflation Scenario

A second baseline simulation was developed that had many features of the first baseline simulation but with much higher inflation rates. Several of the tax alternatives were introduced into this high-inflation scenario to see whether or not the effects of the tax policy would be substantially different if they were introduced at a time when the economy was experiencing a much higher inflation rate than at present.

The high-inflation scenario was generated by assuming that wage rates advanced more rapidly than in the baseline. Since wage rates, and through them unit labor costs, are such a key factor in the inflation outlook in the DRI model, this change alone was sufficient to achieve a very large portion of the desired increase in inflation rates. In addition, a key factor determining industrial commodity prices in the DRI model is a variable that captures delivery delays experienced by purchasing agents. As delivery delays lengthen, industrial prices begin to accelerate due to the shortages that cause the delays. This variable was also increased to capture the acceleration in prices at the wholesale level.

The tax changes embodied in the first and second alternatives (the increase in conventional source taxes, and the BG tax increase) were introduced into the high-inflation scenario in exactly the same fashion as they were in the baseline simulation. The results were then compared to the high-inflation scenario to assess the effect of each tax policy change in the more inflationary environment.

Notes

1. See, for instance, Patric H. Hendershott and Sheng Cheng Hu, "Inflation and Extraordinary Returns on Owner-Occupied Housing: Some Implications for Capital Allocation and Productivity Growth," *Journal of Macroeconomics,* 3 (Spring 1981):177–203.

2. Roger E. Brinner and Stephen H. Brooks, "Stock Prices," in *How Taxes Affect Economic Behavior,* ed. Henry J. Aaron and Joseph A. Pechman (Washington, D.C.: Brookings Institution, 1981) 199–240.

3. E. Hall and D.W. Jorgenson, "Tax Policy and Investment Behavior," *American Economic Review,* 57 (June 1967):391–414.

Appendix C
Alternative Monetary Policy

Table C-1
Gross National Product and the Unemployment Rate

	1987	1989	1991	Six-Year Cumulative
Gross national product (billions current dollars)				
Baseline value	4621.6	5526.1	6596.8	
Difference from baseline (percent)				
Conventional tax increase	0.0	0.0	0.0	0.0
Bradley–Gephardt	0.0	0.0	0.1	0.0
Value-Added Tax	1.0	1.1	1.1	1.1
Consumed-Income Tax	0.0	0.1	−0.3	−0.1
Gross national product (billions of 1972 dollars)				
Baseline value	1775.2	1892.7	2004.1	
Difference from baseline (percent)				
Conventional tax increase	−0.1	−0.2	−0.3	−0.2
Bradley–Gephardt	−0.2	−0.1	−0.1	−0.1
Value-Added Tax	−0.1	−0.2	−0.1	−0.1
Consumed-Income Tax	−0.2	−0.3	−0.5	−0.4
Civilian unemployment rate (percent)				
Baseline value	7.6	7.1	7.0	
Difference from baseline (absolute)				
Conventional tax increase	0.0	0.0	0.1	0.3
Bradley–Gephardt	0.1	0.1	0.0	0.4
Value-Added Tax	0.0	0.1	0.1	0.3
Consumed-Income Tax	0.1	0.2	0.3	1.0

Note: Monetary policy assumption: nominal GNP held on baseline path.

Table C-2
Personal Consumption Expenditures and Saving Rate

	1987	1989	1991	Six-Year Cumulative
Disposable personal income (billions of 1972 dollars)				
Baseline value	1247.4	1317.5	1385.2	
Difference from baseline (percent)				
Conventional tax increase	-1.5	-1.9	-2.0	-1.7
Bradley–Gephardt	-1.8	-1.7	-1.3	-1.6
Value-Added Tax	-1.9	-2.1	-2.2	-2.0
Consumed-Income Tax	-1.6	-2.0	-2.0	-1.8
Consumption expenditures (billions of 1972 dollars)				
Baseline value	1150.4	1216.3	1280.1	
Difference from baseline (percent)				
Conventional tax increase	-0.8	-1.1	-1.3	-1.0
Bradley–Gephardt	-1.2	-1.3	-1.2	-1.1
Value-Added Tax	-1.3	-1.5	-1.6	-1.4
Consumed-Income Tax	-2.3	-3.0	-3.1	-2.6
Durable goods consumption (billions of 1972 dollars)				
Baseline value	194.0	212.2	229.1	
Difference from baseline (percent)				
Conventional tax increase	-1.5	-2.4	-2.8	-2.1
Bradley–Gephardt	-2.4	-2.7	-2.4	-2.4
Value-Added Tax	-3.6	-4.0	-4.3	-3.8
Consumed-Income Tax	-2.7	-3.8	-4.5	-3.5
Nondurable goods consumption (billions of 1972 dollars)				
Baseline value	423.1	438.6	454.4	
Difference from baseline (percent)				
Conventional tax increase	-0.7	-1.1	-1.3	-1.0
Bradley–Gephardt	-1.0	-1.4	-1.4	-1.2
Value-Added Tax	-1.0	-1.3	-1.5	-1.2
Consumed-Income Tax	-2.3	-3.2	-3.4	-2.7
Service consumption (billions of 1972 dollars)				
Baseline value	533.4	565.5	596.6	
Difference from baseline (percent)				
Conventional tax increase	-0.6	-0.7	-0.7	-0.6
Bradley–Gephardt	-0.8	-0.8	-0.6	-0.7
Value-Added Tax	-0.7	-0.7	-0.7	-0.7
Consumed-Income Tax	-2.2	-2.6	-2.4	-2.2
Personal saving rate (percent of disposable income)				
Baseline value	5.0	4.9	4.8	
Difference from baseline (absolute)				
Conventional tax increase	-0.7	-0.8	-0.7	-4.4
Bradley–Gephardt	-0.6	-0.4	-0.1	-2.6
Value-Added Tax	-0.5	-0.6	-0.5	-3.5
Consumed-Income Tax	0.6	1.0	1.2	4.6

Note: Monetary policy assumption: nominal GNP held on baseline path.

Table C-3
Prices, Wages, and Productivity

	1987	1989	1991	Six-Year Cumulative
Implicit price deflator for GNP (1972 = 1.0)				
Baseline value	2.603	2.919	3.291	
Difference from baseline (percent)				
Conventional tax increase	0.1	0.2	0.2	0.1
Bradley–Gephardt	0.2	0.1	0.0	0.1
Value-Added Tax	1.2	1.3	1.3	1.2
Consumed-Income Tax	0.3	0.4	0.2	0.3
Implicit price deflator for consumption (1972 = 1.0)				
Baseline value	2.563	2.868	3.232	
Difference from baseline (percent)				
Conventional tax increase	0.1	0.2	0.3	0.2
Bradley–Gephardt	0.2	0.2	0.0	0.1
Value-Added Tax	1.8	1.9	1.9	1.8
Consumed-Income Tax	0.2	0.3	0.0	0.2
Consumer price index (1967 = 1.0)				
Baseline value	3.650	4.101	4.648	
Difference from baseline (percent)				
Conventional tax increase	0.1	0.2	0.2	0.1
Bradley–Gephardt	0.2	0.2	0.1	0.2
Value-Added Tax	1.9	2.0	1.9	1.9
Consumed-Income Tax	0.2	0.2	0.0	0.1
Hourly compensation (nonfarm business sector, 1977 = 1.0)				
Baseline value	2.070	2.401	2.814	
Difference from baseline (percent)				
Conventional tax increase	0.0	0.0	0.0	0.0
Bradley–Gephardt	0.3	0.2	0.1	0.2
Value-Added Tax	0.6	1.3	1.4	1.0
Consumed-Income Tax	0.0	–0.1	–0.5	–0.2
Productivity per hour (nonfarm business sector, 1977 = 1.0)				
Baseline value	1.110	1.150	1.195	
Difference from baseline (percent)				
Conventional tax increase	0.0	0.1	0.0	0.0
Bradley–Gephardt	–0.1	0.0	0.1	0.0
Value-Added Tax	–0.1	0.0	0.0	0.0
Consumed-Income Tax	0.0	0.1	0.2	0.1

Note: Monetary policy assumption: nominal GNP held on baseline path.

Table C-4
Cost of Business Fixed Capital

	1987	1989	1991	Six-Year Cumulative
Rental price of producers' durable equipment (percent of purchase price)				
Baseline value	0.66	0.71	0.78	
Difference from baseline (absolute)				
Conventional tax increase	0.04	0.05	0.05	0.27
Bradley–Gephardt	0.01	0.02	0.02	0.09
Value-Added Tax	−0.01	−0.01	−0.02	−0.09
Consumed-Income Tax	−0.16	−0.16	−0.16	−0.95
Value of depreciation allowances (equipment)				
Baseline value	0.66	0.66	0.67	
Difference from baseline (absolute)				
Conventional tax increase	0.01	0.01	0.01	0.03
Bradley–Gephardt	−0.04	−0.04	−0.04	−0.25
Value-Added Tax	0.01	0.01	0.01	0.04
Consumed-Income Tax	0.34	0.33	0.33	2.02
Rental price of nonresidential structures (percent of purchase price)				
Baseline value	0.89	0.97	1.08	
Difference from baseline (absolute)				
Conventional tax increase	0.02	0.03	0.03	0.15
Bradley–Gephardt	−0.14	−0.15	−0.16	−0.88
Value-Added Tax	−0.03	−0.04	−0.05	−0.23
Consumed-Income Tax	−0.37	−0.39	−0.42	−2.32
Value of depreciation allowances (structures)				
Baseline value	0.53	0.55	0.56	
Difference from baseline (absolute)				
Conventional tax increase	0.01	0.01	0.01	0.07
Bradley–Gephardt	−0.08	−0.08	−0.08	−0.48
Value-Added Tax	0.01	0.01	0.01	0.08
Consumed-Income Tax	0.47	0.45	0.44	2.73

Note: Monetary policy assumption: nominal GNP held on baseline path.

Table C–5
Business Fixed Investment

	1987	1989	1991	Six-Year Cumulative
Producers' durable equipment investment (billions of 1972 dollars)				
Baseline value	161.9	176.6	190.8	
Difference from baseline (percent)				
Conventional tax increase	-0.3	-0.2	-0.1	-0.2
Bradley–Gephardt	0.4	0.4	-0.1	0.2
Value-Added Tax	0.2	1.2	1.6	0.9
Consumed-Income Tax	0.5	1.6	2.1	1.3
Nonresidential structures investment (billions of 1972 dollars)				
Baseline value	62.3	67.7	72.4	
Difference from baseline (percent)				
Conventional tax increase	-0.2	-0.1	0.0	-0.1
Bradley–Gephardt	2.5	2.8	2.9	2.4
Value-Added Tax	0.8	1.2	1.5	1.1
Consumed-Income Tax	7.6	9.5	10.2	8.1
Business fixed investment (percent of GNP)				
Baseline value	12.0	12.3	12.6	
Difference from baseline (absolute)				
Conventional tax increase	0.0	0.1	0.1	0.4
Bradley–Gephardt	0.2	0.3	0.3	1.5
Value-Added Tax	0.0	0.1	0.2	0.5
Consumed-Income Tax	0.5	0.7	0.8	3.6
Stock of business equipment (billions of 1972 dollars)				
Baseline value	818.1	905.5	994.7	
Difference from baseline (percent)				
Conventional tax increase	0.0	-0.1	-0.1	-0.1
Bradley–Gephardt	0.0	0.2	0.1	0.1
Value-Added Tax	0.0	0.3	0.7	0.3
Consumed-Income Tax	0.0	0.5	1.0	0.4
Stock of business structures (billions of 1972 dollars)				
Baseline value	728.8	775.6	826.7	
Difference from baseline (percent)				
Conventional tax increase	0.0	0.0	0.0	0.0
Bradley–Gephardt	0.2	0.6	0.9	0.5
Value-Added Tax	0.1	0.2	0.4	0.2
Consumed-Income Tax	0.5	1.9	3.2	1.6
Potential GNP (billions of 1972 dollars)				
Baseline value	1926.9	2047.1	2163.3	
Difference from baseline (percent)				
Conventional tax increase	0.0	-0.1	-0.1	0.0
Bradley–Gephardt	0.0	0.1	0.1	0.1
Value-Added Tax	0.0	0.0	0.1	0.0
Consumed-Income Tax	0.0	0.1	0.3	0.1

Note: Monetary policy assumption: nominal GNP held on baseline path.

Table C-6
Federal Expenditures, Revenues, and Deficit

	1987	1989	1991	Six-Year Cumulative
Federal expenditures (billions of dollars)				
Baseline value	1121.1	1316.4	1544.5	
Difference from baseline (absolute)				
Conventional tax increase	−13.2	−24.6	−33.2	−125.6
Bradley–Gephardt	−14.1	−28.8	−42.2	−149.5
Value-Added Tax	−9.5	−19.8	−28.8	−101.5
Consumed-Income Tax	−23.2	−40.3	−53.1	−204.7
Federal revenues (billions of dollars)				
Baseline value	930.4	1145.6	1391.0	
Difference from baseline (absolute)				
Conventional tax increase	45.7	50.6	56.6	297.3
Bradley–Gephardt	40.7	47.2	44.1	264.5
Value-Added Tax	44.5	49.3	56.0	299.7
Consumed-Income Tax	51.7	56.4	52.9	308.7
Surplus or Deficit (−)				
Baseline value	−190.7	−170.8	−153.4	
Difference from baseline (absolute)				
Conventional tax increase	58.9	75.2	89.7	422.9
Bradley–Gephardt	54.8	76.1	86.1	413.9
Value-Added Tax	54.0	69.1	84.8	401.1
Consumed-Income Tax	74.8	96.8	106.0	513.3

Note: Monetary policy assumption: nominal GNP held on baseline path.

Table C-7
Exports and Imports

	1987	1989	1991	Six-Year Cumulative
Exports (billions of 1972 dollars)				
Baseline value	175.2	196.8	221.2	
Difference from baseline (percent)				
Conventional tax increase	0.7	1.6	1.7	1.2
Bradley-Gephardt	0.9	2.2	2.6	1.8
Value-Added Tax	1.2	2.0	2.0	1.6
Consumed-Income Tax	1.4	2.8	2.9	2.3
Imports (billions of 1972 dollars)				
Baseline value	182.7	196.0	210.0	
Difference from baseline (percent)				
Conventional tax increase	-1.1	-2.2	-2.6	-1.8
Bradley-Gephardt	-1.4	-2.7	-3.3	-2.2
Value-Added Tax	-1.8	-2.5	-2.6	-2.1
Consumed-Income Tax	-2.2	-3.9	-3.9	-3.1
Net exports (billions of 1972 dollars)				
Baseline value	-7.5	0.8	11.3	
Difference from baseline (absolute)				
Conventional tax increase	3.3	7.6	9.1	35.2
Bradley-Gephardt	4.2	9.6	12.7	46.1
Value-Added Tax	5.2	9.0	9.9	43.1
Consumed-Income Tax	6.5	13.2	14.7	61.3
Multilateral exchange rate (June 1970 = 1.0)				
Baseline value	0.92	0.89	0.87	
Difference from baseline (percent)				
Conventional tax increase	-2.4	-3.6	-3.2	-2.9
Bradley-Gephardt	-3.0	-4.9	-5.3	-4.1
Value-Added Tax	-3.4	-4.3	-4.0	-3.7
Consumed-Income Tax	-4.9	-5.9	-4.5	-4.8

Note: Monetary policy assumption: nominal GNP held on baseline path.

Table C-8
Interest Rates, Money, and Velocity

	1987	1989	1991	Six-Year Cumulative
Three-month treasury bill rate (percent)				
Baseline value	8.41	7.80	7.06	
Difference from baseline (absolute)				
Conventional tax increase	-1.14	-1.06	-0.95	-6.71
Bradley–Gephardt	-1.50	-1.49	-1.45	-9.23
Value-Added Tax	-1.76	-1.50	-1.39	-8.98
Consumed-Income Tax	-2.78	-1.52	-0.92	-12.53
New issue rate—high-grade corporate bonds (percent)				
Baseline value	11.68	10.83	10.41	
Difference from baseline (absolute)				
Conventional tax increase	0.02	0.05	0.03	0.16
Bradley–Gephardt	0.03	0.00	-0.02	-0.02
Value-Added Tax	0.26	0.14	0.03	0.95
Consumed-Income Tax	0.08	0.15	0.06	0.46
Money supply, M1 (billions of dollars)				
Baseline value	644.9	721.0	807.5	
Difference from baseline (percent)				
Conventional tax increase	0.5	0.4	0.4	0.4
Bradley–Gephardt	0.4	0.1	-0.2	0.2
Value-Added Tax	1.3	1.3	1.3	1.3
Consumed-Income Tax	0.9	0.7	0.3	0.7
Velocity of money (gross national product divided by money, M1)				
Baseline value	7.17	7.66	8.17	
Difference from baseline (percent)				
Conventional tax increase	-0.5	-0.5	-0.4	-0.5
Bradley–Gephardt	-0.4	-0.1	0.3	-0.2
Value-Added Tax	-0.3	-0.2	-0.2	-0.2
Consumed-Income Tax	-0.9	-0.6	-0.6	-0.8

Note: Monetary policy assumption: nominal GNP held on baseline path.

Table C-9

Components of National Saving and Investment

(billions of dollars)

	1987	1989	1991	Six-Year Cumulative
Total saving (billions of dollars)				
Baseline value	663.8	823.7	1003.6	
Difference from baseline (absolute)				
Conventional tax increase	17.4	26.2	36.8	142.6
Bradley–Gephardt	23.8	37.7	49.9	195.7
Value-Added Tax	31.5	43.8	62.5	255.6
Consumed-Income Tax	57.4	98.7	113.2	454.6
Private saving				
Baseline value	791.1	920.0	1074.6	
Difference from baseline (absolute)				
Conventional tax increase	-37.6	-43.8	-45.7	-249.6
Bradley–Gephardt	-18.3	-27.6	-22.8	-148.1
Value-Added Tax	-14.4	-16.9	-11.3	-96.7
Consumed-Income Tax	-8.2	9.7	19.0	0.8
Personal saving				
Baseline value	159.4	184.0	214.2	
Difference from baseline (absolute)				
Conventional tax increase	-24.5	-31.5	-34.1	-175.7
Bradley–Gephardt	-21.5	-17.4	-7.2	-103.8
Value-Added Tax	-16.6	-24.1	-25.0	-128.5
Consumed-Income Tax	18.2	33.7	46.8	158.3
Corporate saving				
Baseline value	631.8	736.0	860.4	
Difference from baseline (absolute)				
Conventional tax increase	-13.1	-12.3	-11.5	-73.9
Bradley–Gephardt	3.2	-10.2	-15.6	-44.3
Value-Added Tax	2.2	7.2	13.6	31.7
Consumed-Income Tax	-26.3	-24.0	-27.8	-157.5
Government saving				
Baseline value	-127.4	-96.4	-71.0	
Difference from baseline (absolute)				
Conventional tax increase	55.0	70.0	82.5	392.3
Bradley–Gephardt	42.1	65.3	72.7	343.8
Value-Added Tax	45.9	60.7	73.9	352.3
Consumed-Income Tax	65.6	89.0	94.2	453.8
Total investment (billions of dollars)				
Baseline value	658.6	819.8	999.3	
Difference from baseline (absolute)				
Conventional tax increase	17.4	26.1	36.8	142.5
Bradley–Gephardt	23.6	37.5	49.7	194.8
Value-Added Tax	31.5	43.8	62.5	255.4
Consumed-Income Tax	57.2	98.6	113.1	453.8

Table C-9 continued

	1987	1989	1991	Six-Year Cumulative
Domestic investment				
Baseline value	784.8	955.9	1147.5	
Difference from baseline (absolute)				
Conventional tax increase	14.6	15.0	16.4	86.0
Bradley–Gephardt	19.6	25.1	27.7	132.3
Value-Added Tax	23.1	27.1	39.0	172.6
Consumed-Income Tax	49.0	73.4	71.7	325.6
Business Fixed Investment				
Baseline value	552.6	679.8	830.9	
Difference from baseline (absolute)				
Conventional tax increase	0.6	4.3	6.8	20.1
Bradley–Gephardt	10.1	17.4	20.4	84.3
Value-Added Tax	5.4	14.7	21.2	72.0
Consumed-Income Tax	21.8	40.2	50.6	196.2
Residential Investment				
Baseline value	193.9	232.9	268.7	
Difference from baseline (absolute)				
Conventional tax increase	14.5	11.8	11.1	69.5
Bradley–Gephardt	10.7	8.1	5.9	46.2
Value-Added Tax	19.0	11.9	16.7	97.5
Consumed-Income Tax	27.7	34.8	24.9	138.9
Inventory Investment				
Baseline value	38.3	43.2	47.8	
Difference from baseline (absolute)				
Conventional tax increase	−0.6	−1.2	−1.6	−3.7
Bradley–Gephardt	−1.2	−0.4	1.4	1.8
Value-Added Tax	−1.2	0.5	1.1	3.1
Consumed-Income Tax	−0.6	−1.5	−3.8	−9.5
Foreign				
Baseline value	−126.3	−136.1	−148.2	
Difference from baseline (absolute)				
Conventional tax increase	2.8	11.2	20.4	56.5
Bradley–Gephardt	4.0	12.4	21.9	62.5
Value-Added Tax	8.3	16.6	23.5	82.8
Consumed-Income Tax	8.2	25.2	41.4	128.2

Note: Monetary policy assumption: nominal GNP held on baseline path.

Index

About the Authors

Paul V. Teplitz is a senior consultant at Cambridge Research Institute, a management consulting firm in Cambridge, Massachusetts. With a background in economic and industry analysis, he specializes in corporate strategy and organization. In addition, he has consulted with corporate clients in regulatory proceedings and antitrust litigation.

Dr. Teplitz graduated from the Massachusetts Institute of Technology in 1962 and received the doctorate in business administration from Harvard University in 1969. Before entering consulting, he held engineering and corporate planning positions at M.I.T. His books include *Urban Analysis* (coauthor), *Trends Affecting the U.S. Banking System*, and *Baseball Economics and Public Policy* (coauthor).

Stephen H. Brooks is a consultant to Cambridge Research Institute and president of S.H. Brooks and Company, a firm specializing in applications of macroeconomics and econometric modeling.

Dr. Brooks graduated from Harvard University in 1972 and received the Ph.D. from the University of Michigan in 1980. He has held positions as senior staff economist at the President's Council of Economic Advisers and as senior economist at Data Resources, Inc. In addition to his consulting activities, he writes frequent columns on economics for New England Business magazine.